'I am delighted to endorse this wonderful book. It is filled with insights and provocative questions and is beautifully written. The stories offer a look into the complexity coaches and leaders alike face in unravelling the challenges and interactions in the world of organizations. Amanda's transparency regarding her own journey is an inspiring lesson in the importance of openness and honesty in leading a life of integrity and facilitating clients.'

Wendy Palmer, author of *Leadership Embodiment*

'As I read this wonderful offering, I found myself richly transported into a gentle journey of leadership and discovery. Amanda's words are a precious portal to contemplation that deepens reflection and challenges fixed perceptions of how to approach leadership practice. Her rich blend of personal narrative and powerful insights invites the reader to honor learning anew and embrace a different view of what was thought known. This book is truly a gift from the heart.'

Zachary Green, PhD, Professor of Practice, Leadership Studies, University of San Diego

'A natural storyteller, Amanda generously shares her humanness so we might navigate an understanding of how we show up in similar situations. She calls us, with kindness, to inquire more, to listen harder and to appreciate others for all they are as much as we appreciate ourselves.

Amanda is an artist with a gift that paints pictures in her writing; images that truly bring the concepts she offers to life in a spectacular, 3-dimensional way, encouraging reflection and challenge to dig deep and bring our authentic selves forward. This book is a guide and companion that will sit alongside us every day as we consider what is important.'

Tania Watson, Founder, Creative Coaching Limited

'As we drift towards challenges that will deeply affect the ways in which we live, work and think together, Amanda offers a series of contemplations and gentle provocations which encourage readers to extend the quality of their leadership range and repertoire. In bringing her 'whole self' to her writing and reflective practice, Amanda offers both her successes and failures; moments when her deep investment in dialogue has been beneficial and others which remain troublesome and unresolved. As she lives her questions, we can be accompanied and supported by her narratives, and better resourced to meet the future.'

Dr. Steve Marshall, Writer and Photographer, www.drstevemarshall.com

'This is a wonderful collection of writings that gently invite us into our own reflections on practice. The power of this book lies in its simplicity. There is a real ease in Amanda's writing that, as a reader, enables me to access something deeper within myself.'

Dr. Eunice Aquilina, author of *Embodying Authenticity*

Weekly Leadership Contemplations

Amanda Ridings

Copyright © 2024 Amanda Ridings

The moral right of the author has been asserted.

First published in 2020 by:

Matador
Unit E2, Airfield Business Park
Harrison Rd
Market Harborough
Leicestershire LE16 7UL

Matador is an imprint of Troubador Publishing Ltd: https://www.troubador.co.uk

Published in 2024 by Originate Books

Originate Books is an imprint of Originate: www.originate.org.uk

Printed by IngramSpark

ISBN 978-1-0686609-5-5

Also available as an e-book: ISBN 978-1-0686609-6-2

Apart from any fair dealing for the purposes of research or private study, or criticism or review, as permitted under the Copyright, Designs and Patents Act 1988, this publication may only be reproduced, stored or transmitted, in any form or by any means, with the prior permission in writing of the publishers, or in the case of reprographic reproduction in accordance with the terms of licences issued by the Copyright Licensing Agency. Enquiries concerning reproduction outside those terms should be sent to the publishers, Originate Books.

British Library Cataloguing in Publication Data.

A catalogue record for this book is available from the British Library.

This book is dedicated to the memory of my father and mother, John Ridings (1935-2002) and Lucy Ridings (née Chaloner, 1935-1979).

Any good within me is a tribute to them.

'... have patience with everything unresolved in your heart and to try to love the questions themselves as if they were locked rooms or books written in a very foreign language. Don't search for the answers, which could not be given to you now, because you would not be able to live them. And the point is to live everything. Live the questions now. Perhaps then, someday far in the future, you will gradually, without even noticing it, live your way into the answer.'[1]

Rainer Maria Rilke

CONTENTS

Preface: An invitation to reflect on your leadership	10
Self-leadership	12
1 Beginning again…	14
2 Being faithless	16
3 Choice of attention	18
4 Sailing through	20
5 Stories we tell ourselves	22
6 Clarity and charity	24
7 Self-doubt	26
8 Falling short	28
9 Perfect whole	30
10 Dressing down	32
11 Energetic cheques	34
12 System upgrades	36
13 Letter from Falkland	38
Leadership in conversations	40
14 Beyond words	42
15 Handing over	44
16 Energy rising	46

17 The grittiness of dialogue	48
18 Gravitational pull	50
19 Holding conversations	52
20 Voice recognition	54
21 Beyond belief	56
22 Attention!	58
23 Naked truth	60
24 Sounds of silence	62
25 Conversation operating systems	64
26 Letter from Assynt	66
Leadership perspectives	**68**
27 Gaining perspective	70
28 The vision thing	72
29 Quiet industry	74
30 Gradients of change	76
31 Contemplating activism	78
32 Changing minds	80
33 Passing places	82
34 Crafting intention	84
35 Careless talk	86
36 Ethical edges	88
37 Light and shade	90
38 Rhythms and rests	92
39 Letter from Holy Isle	94

Leading and learning — 96

- 40 Mind-taming update — 98
- 41 Sweet spot for support — 100
- 42 Raising questions — 102
- 43 Mind the gap — 104
- 44 Practice-based learning — 106
- 45 Coming through — 108
- 46 A gift of five days — 110
- 47 The silent treatment — 112
- 48 Back to basics — 114
- 49 (DK)squared — 116
- 50 Time in — 118
- 51 Season of goodwill — 120
- 52 Letter from Bhutan — 122

Coda: Rejoicing — 126

- Key terms and what I mean by them — 128
- Acknowledgements and gratitude — 131
- References — 132
- About the author — 134

Preface: An invitation to reflect on your leadership

Written in September 2015

The question most asked about my first book *Pause for Breath*[2] is: how long did it take to write? The tongue-in-cheek answer is fifty-two years, my age when it was published. The more representative answer is three years, the period when my writing focused on the topic of leadership conversations.

People then ask about my next book. For ages I swore there wouldn't be another because, although I'd enjoyed actually writing the book, the detailed attention required for the production process was draining. Despite this, I continued to write and, in 2012, began posting articles on my website.[3] I relished the discipline of crafting short pieces and the freedom to choose my subject matter. Gradually, I reconnected with my pleasure in writing.

As the number of blog posts increased, an idea took shape: I would curate a collection of them and publish a book to support reflection about leadership in all its forms. The result is in your hands.

The invitation of this book is to select one piece each week and read it several times, using it to stimulate reflection on your experiences and the choices you make as you go about your life and work. The pieces are deliberately short to support this and, over a week, you might:

1 Use the reflective questions that follow each article to prompt a personal inquiry into the matters raised: what is evoked in you?

2 More generally ponder connections between my narrative and your experiences in work or life: what resonates and what doesn't?

3 Pay attention to the process of re-reading: what changes? Do different things catch your attention? What do you tend to skip over?

The book is set out in four sections: self-leadership; leadership in conversations; leadership perspectives; and leading and learning. My intention is that each piece can be read independently, but there are links between some and I've done my best to signpost these when they occur. At the end of the book, I've also provided a brief description of some of the terms I use and the meaning I attribute to them.

The pieces are prompted by my personal experiences of challenge and growth and by thought-provoking themes brought to my attention by clients or events in the world around me. In my work as an executive coach and coach supervisor, I'm privileged to walk alongside leaders and practitioners as they struggle to make good choices in an increasingly complex world. I'm inspired by the questions they raise and the care they bring to reflecting on their thinking, words and actions. And, in my own learning, I've become acutely aware that the greatest growth often arises from the 'gap' between my aspirations and my ability to live up to them.

Over time, I've come to believe that personal development doesn't depend on acquiring more knowledge, tools and techniques. Instead, it rests on increasing our capacity to put what we know into practice, especially when the chips are down. Our ability to contribute skilfully and effectively, as leaders and human beings, is determined by our character and the quality of our motivation. This inner spirit flavours what we say and do, influencing everything in our field. This premise is at the heart of the weekly leadership contemplations.

As you read, you will notice recurring themes. These represent my personal preoccupations with leadership and leadership development in the 21st century. The book is not researched in any way and doesn't represent a particular leadership framework. Where I've drawn on the work of others I've done my utmost to credit them. However, it is possible that I've inadvertently used a phrase, word or motif that others claim as theirs. My intent is only to share my experiences and prompt reflection; if I have adopted your words without acknowledgement then it is simply because I am unaware of your material. If you let me know, I will put it right.

Self-leadership

Whether we aspire to transform systems, create new things or support others to realise their potential, our impact depends on the quality and integrity of our internal architecture, the deeply coded beliefs, values, principles, knowledge, experiences and ethics that guide what we do and say. Awareness of these inner structures enables us to be more deliberate in the way we carry ourselves. This section explores these themes.

Beginning again…

Being faithless

Choice of attention

Sailing through

Stories we tell ourselves

Clarity and charity

Self-doubt

Falling short

Perfect whole

Dressing down

Energetic cheques

System upgrades

Letter from Falkland

1 Beginning again...
Written in January 2013

In preparation for a trip of a lifetime to Bhutan, I took up running – again! I've only ever run short distances and I'm pretty slow. When I was younger, I ran regularly for a while, until an illness intervened. In returning to health, I concentrated on low-impact exercise such as swimming and T'ai Chi Ch'üan. In my fifties, this seemed sensible.

Two things changed. My local pool closed for eighteen months and I swapped swimming for walking, enjoying the early mornings in the beautiful Fife countryside. Then I realised I'd need to develop my stamina to enjoy walking at altitude in Bhutan and it seemed natural to swap walking for running on some days.

Unsure of my fitness, I experimented with short intervals of running during a walk. I ached the next day but wasn't incapacitated. I'd pitched it about right. Repeating the process a couple of days later, it was a little easier. More confident, I could focus on breathing, pacing and alignment. On subsequent outings, I slowly built my endurance and refined my technique.

In rediscovering running, I became aware of the parallels with changing practice in conversations, linked to my dialogue-related work: I *know* how to run – I've been able to execute the required physical movements from a young age. Similarly, I *know* how to participate in conversations – I've been doing it for more than fifty years.

Yet *knowing* how to run has limits, as my body quickly tells me. If I run unskilfully, on uneven terrain or beyond my current fitness levels, I feel pain and/or become breathless. Unless I adjust my pace, posture or breathing, I'll soon be exhausted. Further, without regular practice, I won't improve my stamina. It's obvious! Yet for years I didn't make the connection between this and increasing my level of 'fitness' for remaining calm and resourceful in my interactions with others.

Self-leadership

While our body quickly tells us when we've overdone it physically, it can be harder to recognise that we've overstretched ourselves in a fraught conversation. The signs are more subtle: we may experience dissatisfaction, irritation or frustration, or feel we've been ignored or silenced. Further, we may be tempted to explain away any discomfort or unease – the emotional or cognitive equivalent to aching muscles – by attributing it to other people, or to circumstances.

By ignoring these signs, or discounting their importance, we excuse ourselves from examining our own part in what's taking place. While this may assuage our pride, it denies us an opportunity to learn and to change our approach.

With running, I didn't have the luxury of ignoring the signs that I'd overextended my fitness. Beginning to enjoy the freedom of running, I overdid it, but the first I knew of this was the next morning, when I felt the painful impact in my ageing hips. I didn't run again for a week. This was frustrating, but my body gave me no alternative. If I wanted to continue running, I had to rest and then… *begin again*.

To begin again, the motivation for building skill and capacity needs to be greater than any dent to a fragile ego. My desire to enjoy walking at altitude in Bhutan outweighed the temptation to give up something I was struggling with, and so I began again. This is the true discipline of practice-based learning. When we try to add to our leadership repertoire by trying out new approaches, we'll inevitably encounter setbacks or self-doubt as we venture into unfamiliar terrain. When this happens, what will support us to begin again?

Contemplations

- Think of a time when you intended to make a change in your leadership practice but were unable to see it through. What deterred you? What can you learn from this?
- In contrast, if you've been able to successfully establish a different approach, what enabled you to sustain your effort?

2 Being faithless

Written in July 2014

On my office wall, there is a piece of paper containing an extract from a poem that acts as a call to arms about the choices I make and the extent to which I'm able to be true to self and risk disappointing others. The verse comes from *The Invitation*[4] by Oriah Mountain Dreamer and can be summarised as:

> *'I want to know... if you can be faithless and therefore trustworthy.'*

The words remind me that the choices we make depend on *what* and *who* matters to us. We can be faithless to one call on our time and attention in order to be true to another. Perhaps we are completely trustworthy in giving precedence to our family and so appear faithless to work or social occasions. Or perhaps we keep faith primarily with our work – and our relationships suffer, despite the material benefits and security we provide for the long term.

Whatever our priorities, it helps to be clear about them and to make conscious choices in accordance with them. In a frenetic world, the sheer number and variety of calls on our time precludes the possibility of saying 'yes' to them all. Given this, how do we determine what we accept and what we decline?

It can be tough to say 'no' – when we care about our relationship with the person asking something of us, we may worry about upsetting them or letting them down. There may be financial consequences if we say 'no', or perhaps we don't want to break a promise or be seen as selfish or unreliable. So we might say a reluctant or resentful 'yes' – or say nothing, to avoid saying 'no'.

Without 'no' in our repertoire, we risk becoming overextended, or even overwhelmed, by the commitments we've made. A lack of capacity to be faithless *squeezes* other aspects of life, such as time with family, or resourcing activities such as sport, art, gardening...

Yet being faithless is uncomfortable. This makes it hard to say 'no' *gracefully* which, in turn, influences how that 'no' is received. Paradoxically, the more I'm caught up in what others will think, the greater the likelihood I'll be clumsy or unskilful and so adversely affect the relationships concerned.

The very real difficulty of saying 'no' with elegance and warmth is an invitation to practise doing so.

When I decline a request, I strongly believe a sincere and skilful 'no' will, in the long run, be better than a grudging or inauthentic 'yes'. So, what helps me put this into practice?

Two things that support us to say 'no' with poise are:

- Being clear about what we're *being true to*, so we understand how our 'no' allows us to be trustworthy; and
- Using centring or mindfulness practices to settle into a sense of calm composure, so that we say 'no' from this place without wondering how it might be received.

In understanding what we're being true to and seeking to balance our own interests with those of others, a 'no' can become a positive intention to honour something that's important.

If we're not faithful enough to our own priorities, we risk compressing our unique contribution to the world into increasingly smaller spaces. In doing so, we impoverish our spirit – something essential, nourishing and enriching gets lost. We betray ourselves for our lack of capacity to disappoint another. We also deny the world the best of ourselves.

Contemplations

- In what circumstances have you said 'yes' when you'd rather have said 'no'? What made 'no' difficult? In saying 'yes', what have you been faithless to?
- How might you say 'no' more often and more elegantly? What will a skilful 'no' free you up to do?

3 Choice of attention
Written in August 2014

In today's world we're bombarded by sensory stimuli – things to see, hear, touch. Alongside this, we're exposed to large volumes of cognitive and emotional data with associated relational complexities. If we were to pay attention to everything, we'd quickly become overwhelmed. So, how do we decide where to put our attention? How do we separate important and/or relevant matters from the background noise? To what extent do we make such choices consciously?

These questions arose in sharp focus during some meditation training, in which we were practising following our breath. In this activity, the *quality* of attention matters, placing it on the breath in a manner that isn't too heavy or light. Even in a quiet and supportive setting, my attempts to simply rest my attention on my breath were ineffectual.

This demonstrated that, even with a process as crucial as breathing, if it is undramatic and routine, attention is likely to drift. Assuming I'm in good health and in a safe setting, breathing is mundane. It doesn't naturally *hold* my attention. It requires effort to remain engaged with something that I know is significant, yet find unexciting.

And it makes me wonder what we may be discounting in our daily settings, which are often not quiet and supportive. When we're inundated by emails, texts, twitter feeds, social media updates, voicemail, phone calls, Skype – not to mention more traditional paperwork and meetings – what do we neglect simply because it seems uninteresting or because it isn't actively demanding our immediate attention?

It's never been more important to make *deliberate choices* about where we place our attention. The poet WH Auden wrote:

'Choice of attention – to pay attention to this and to ignore that – is to the inner life what choice of action is to the outer. In both cases a person is responsible for their choice and must accept the consequences.'

In choosing what to attend to, we encounter two challenges:

- Distinguishing that which is essential from the welter of stuff that is unimportant but may be superficially more alluring; and then…
- Ensuring that our attention remains with what matters.

In leadership, it's relatively easy to become clear about our purpose and priorities, yet we repeatedly find ourselves investing time in the trivial. To be mindful about which calls on our attention are relevant and which are not, we need to understand how and why we get distracted. However, when we *candidly* examine why we get caught up in non-essential things, we may find that we're avoiding activities we find uncomfortable, unpleasant or difficult. Or perhaps we're choosing something that provides a short-term boost of pleasure or wellbeing that we justify on the basis of all the hard work we put in. Or perhaps we fear we'll miss out if we're not constantly plugged in to the news, social media or office gossip.

With reflection, we may be able to clarify why we attend to *this* and disregard *that*. With this awareness and with practice, it's possible to become more mindful of the whereabouts of our attention and to be more deliberate in where it rests. We might also consider how tightly or loosely we focus on an issue. If the quality of our attention is too loose, we can be easily distracted. If it is too tight, we lose peripheral vision or perspective. What is the quality of attention that allows us to stay with an issue, yet remain aware of our environment and context?

Contemplations

- When have you missed an important detail because your attention has been caught up in something more interesting?
- When you look closely, what is in play when you become distracted? How does this awareness help you to focus on what matters, even when it is unexciting?

4 Sailing through
Written in May 2015

It's many, many years since I crewed a sailing dinghy, but recently the experience came flooding back. I loved being on the water, feeling the hull move under my feet and shifting my weight to help balance the boat for optimum speed and stability. I enjoyed 'hiking' out over the side on windy days. My favourite part, though, was 'playing' the spinnaker – trimming the billowing third sail used when the wind was aft. While I didn't much enjoy *racing* dinghies, the visceral memories of sailing thrill me still.

The reminder of these experiences came during a Leadership Embodiment retreat with Wendy Palmer.[23] We were exploring what happens when our ideas (or actions) meet resistance. While there are several archetypal patterns of behaviour in these circumstances, such as backing off, or getting stuck, we were focusing on the occasions we choose to *press our point*, despite opposition. Often we tense as we do this, perhaps girding our loins or digging in, physically hunching to prepare for a struggle. Bracing in this way, we're likely to perpetuate (and even increase) resistance to what we're saying.

On the retreat, we were exploring an alternative: reorganising our physiology and energy to focus on a bigger, more inclusive picture. To do this we practised accessing a sense of uplifted, open presence and placing our attention beyond the opposing energy. When centred and at ease, we are able to move forward in an inspired and inspiring way. It is as if the opposition melts away. In addition, I find that when I connect to and speak for a greater purpose, I also melt away. My sense of 'me' diminishes and I become part of a larger movement that includes alternative views.

In the debrief, one of the group asked if it was more helpful to concentrate on a sense of uplift, or on going forward. Suddenly, I was back in a dinghy, raising the spinnaker, watching it fill with wind and feeling the bow of the boat lift slightly and surge forward. I get a similar sense of exhilaration when this particular practice comes together. When my motivation is to benefit others, a 'breeze' of their collective energy supports me to *sail through* difficulties.

When the practice doesn't come together, what then? Perhaps opposition or resistance intensifies as I attempt to strong-arm my way through it. Or perhaps it folds under the power of my conviction.

Playing out these patterns *bodily* reveals the psychological and emotional impact of trying to impose my agenda on others. A conviction that 'I'm right' includes a subtle corollary: 'you're wrong'. Though unspoken, the energy of this message can provoke an instinctive pushback (I'm *not* wrong!) or unthinking agreement or retreat (I'm wrong, *as usual*). If, instead, I can acknowledge and include the perspectives of others and find a shared purpose or motivation, it may be possible to move forward *together*.

'Sailing through' is an inspiring option, which is easy to imagine but hard to do. It took me three years to be able to fully embody this physical practice. And still, when I teach it, the added pressure of demonstrating sometimes means I don't quite do it justice.

However, what is most important to me is that I transfer the learning from the simulator of embodied activities in a workshop into real interactions with others. The question is: when I find myself in conflict, tensed into my signature *reaction* to resistance, can I transform my energetic presence and access a more resourceful *response* to the situation?

The truthful answer is: sometimes. This is progress!

Contemplations

- What is your typical reaction when someone opposes your view, or takes action at odds with your expectations? What are your go-to thoughts? What sensations occur in your body?

- What do you lose sight of when you're caught up in this reaction? How does it limit your effectiveness with others? What strategies can you draw on to help you reconnect with the bigger picture?

5 Stories we tell ourselves

Written in September 2013

What is your story in this moment? How does it influence what you believe to be possible?

Trainer and coach Judy Ringer[5] speaks of 'good reality' and 'bad reality', describing how the same circumstances can look very different after a break and/or some rest. Even if we understand the *bias* of spin and the *unreality* of reality TV, we can overlook the need to question things we regard to be fact in our immediate circumstances. We often forget to ask: what is *really* happening here?

In exploring dialogue practices with a senior team, a familiar pattern emerged. They wanted to examine how they talked together and find ways to work more collaboratively. As is usual, they had diverse priorities and styles and a tendency to be critical of each other. There was friction between their departments and, when things went awry, blame was quickly attributed.

As we touched on some of their differences, one team member described a customer's frustration with a department led by one of his colleagues: they had failed to deliver a key input on time. Getting into his stride, he was scathing about the inadequacies of the team responsible. The leader of the team being criticised tried to interject with questions of clarification. She believed that all the customer's requirements had been met and on time. Further, she was angry about the censure of her team.

Whoever was 'right', it was clear that the team member leading the attack had taken the customer's perspective at face value, rather than saying 'let me look into that for you'. Influenced by a cultural narrative of discord and blame, he accepted the customer's allegation and joined in with the condemnation of part of his organisation.

It became apparent that this kind of behaviour wasn't confined to a single member of the senior team. Across the organisation, there was an unhesitating readiness to find fault with others when things went wrong, particularly when adverse feedback came from outside. The senior team all contributed to this pattern to some degree.

When there seem to be two or more sides to a story, it's helpful to understand how we create our 'reality'. The human mind is necessarily selective about what it takes into account. We cannot possibly take in and make sense of all the sensory data that is available to us in any moment. Based on sensory preferences, past experiences, our beliefs and other elements of our unique personal architecture, our brain *filters* what we highlight or discount.

Using incomplete data, we draw quick conclusions by rifling through our library of experiences in order to find a useful template for whatever we're facing. This is efficient and, mostly, *good enough*. However, it does mean we can overlook potential pitfalls and rely on our rapid assessment to create a story that we treat as fact. Each time we re-tell the story it becomes more solid, more certain. Confidence in our single truth reduces our capacity for different interpretations – we become stuck in *one side* of a story.

There is never one 'truth' in exchanges between people. If we accept this, we ensure we *triangulate* any narrative and seek a third perspective on events. In my example, the senior team agreed to be more *generous* to each other and give *the benefit of the doubt* to colleagues when a part of the organisation was slated. They committed to asking those directly affected by a criticism for *their* perspective before forming a judgement and/or taking action.

Contemplations

- What influences whether you see things in a positive or negative light? How can you check your experience?
- When you express (seemingly justified) irritation at the incompetence of colleagues, what prevents you from checking *their* reality?

Clarity and charity
Written in April 2015

For years I've had a literary crush on the Scottish writer and poet Andrew Greig.[6] He writes evocatively of landscape and perceptively about people. Reading his work, my mind eases into a warm bath of words. My devotion extended to reading his books about golf[7] and fishing[8], even though I couldn't imagine enjoying them, having negligible interest in these subjects.

As it turns out, both books are contemplative explorations of life. *Preferred Lies*,[7] ostensibly about golf, is a moving narrative about Greig's return to health after serious illness, full of insights on the complexities of being human. In golf, the term 'prefer the lie' means to improve the position of an unplayable ball. Greig exploits the ambiguity of the words to riff on the lies we prefer in life, the little adjustments we make to embellish or edit the way we interpret the world, often without noticing.

I returned to the book recently, prompted by a seam of coaching clients who claimed they were unable to trust a colleague 'because they *lie*'. It's unusual for this to be declared so bluntly, even within a confidential space. The client narratives were different, but each touched on truth, lies, memory and the spin we put on things.

One client wondered who to believe when she heard different accounts of a conversation from the two people involved. She was inclined to favour one version of events, judging the other to be rooted in a desire to save face or be seen in a good light. In crediting one version of events as accurate, the other became deceitful, with an implication of deliberate dishonesty.

I wondered about this exacting standard of truth. I'm sure I'm not alone in being careful how I present my credentials and experience to secure a job. In accentuating strengths and skipping over perceived shortcomings, am I being economical with the truth, giving a positive spin or lying?

Drawing on the dialogue practice of suspending judgement, I began to probe the client's construct of lying. I invited her to reflect on occasions when she had emphasised or downplayed an event or attribute in order to influence someone's opinion. We also talked about how each person experiences the world in a partial and somewhat arbitrary way. And our memories can be faulty.

For example, I recently told a doctor I'd had my wisdom teeth removed in a Dundee hospital. I was *very* convincing. Later, I checked. The teeth were extracted a year before my family moved to Scotland. Despite this knowledge, my mind still prefers the lie of Dundee to the reality of Shropshire.

Then I found myself stretching a truth in a social setting, to bolster my reputation. Separately, I submitted a resumé for some work which, I later discovered, claimed membership of a professional body which had lapsed. Two lies: the first being one of commission, unknown to the recipient; the second a genuine oversight, but in a formal context. I corrected the latter, to be seen to be truthful. I let the other lie.

So, when I encounter approximations of the truth, I'm reluctant to throw stones. Instead, I seek to apply *'clarity and charity'* (Greig again). In terms of clarity, can I see another person clearly, in their full human incoherence of desires and doubts, strengths and shortfalls? In terms of charity, can I be honest and say 'they're just like me'?

If I can be clear-sighted and generous of spirit, I'm more able to be curious about context and motivation. If I inquire, I may find a deeper truth.

Contemplations

- While fabricating a story may be one extreme, and forgetful omission another, where in the spectrum of perception do you believe truth ends and lies begin?
- When faced with an inner conflict, what values determine the lie you prefer?

7 Self-doubt

Written in August 2012

A year after the publication of my first book, *Pause for Breath*,[2] it received an international award, offering an opportunity to reprint, with a new cover. This also allowed me to do a further edit, since I seemed to find a new typo every time I opened the first edition.

I approached the review with trepidation. I hadn't read my book since it came out. The process of design and production had exhausted my interest in it. Despite having great people around me, I had to focus on details, checking and re-checking changes, which is not my strength. In the repetitive reading and editing, I experienced a kind of white-out, or word-blindness, losing any capacity for judging the quality of the writing. A year later, I was nervous about picking it up again: what if it was, after all, rubbish?

Doubts of this kind crop up frequently in coaching. Despite positive feedback and tangible results, many clients question the value of what they do, or the quality of their leadership.

To understand how and why such questions arise, it can be helpful to examine the nature of our internal dialogue, the thoughts, feelings, memories and ideas that comprise our inner conversation. One method for doing this is to use a metaphor of three reference points: head, heart and gut. In facing a predicament, we might ask:

- Head: What is my *thinking* about this? What judgements, ideas, perceptions are in play?

- Heart: What *feelings and values* are present? What are my hopes and fears for different courses of action and how others might respond?

- Gut: What matters, deep down? What do I *sense* is important, in the bigger schemes of things?

In untangling internal dialogue, it's important to acknowledge each inner voice, regarding them all as legitimate. Each represents an important aspect of our experience. If we're able to embrace them all, they will distil into what really matters.

For example, in my internal dialogue about re-reading *Pause for Breath*,[2] I noted that my head recognised the evidence: the book had been well-received. However, in my heart I was still seeking reassurance and further approval. The book isn't to everyone's taste and, as my heart went into writing it, it was (and remains) easy to give credence to the comments of detractors and wonder if they are right. At the time, supporters seemed to be mainly friends and associates and they might just have been humouring me!

In my gut, I found the seat of my fear: I might now judge the book to be awful, despite the independent affirmation of its value. However, I also reconnected with my *purpose* in writing the book: to share experiences and learning that had been useful for me and which I hoped would benefit others. I also intended that it would support my dialogue-related work.

By separating out and examining the different strands of my internal dialogue, I could see that my reasoning about the merits of my book was undermined by both a lack of trust in others and high expectations of myself. My doubts were more about my personal fragility than the quality of my writing.

Being reminded of my original intentions provided enough motivation to set aside my insecurities and self-doubt and re-engage with the book. I had an opportunity to improve it and perhaps make it of even greater benefit to others. And so I read it again – and was pleasantly surprised.

Contemplations

- When do you doubt yourself, *despite evidence to the contrary*? What is that about?
- Recall a specific example of self-doubt and examine your internal dialogue using the framework of head, heart and gut. What becomes clearer?

8 Falling short

Written in June 2015

The warmth of summer briefly reached Fife for a few days before cool conditions returned. Windy and cloudy, the early summer weather has taken its toll on my raspberry bushes. Currently knee-high, they've usually reached shoulder-height by this time of year. They're trying to flower, whereas the norm would be a crop of rapidly expanding berries.

In this *failure* to blossom and fruit to schedule, I've not once thought 'what kind of a raspberry bush are you?!' or otherwise judged the performance of these trusted producers of delicious berries. I *know* that their capacity to deliver depends on soil, sunlight, warmth, bees and rain. I understand that they're unable to reach their potential in the current conditions.

So, when I witness my clients judging themselves for falling short in some way, I tell them about my raspberries. They laugh, because it *is* ridiculous to berate a bush. Yet they baulk at extending a similar generosity of spirit to self (and/or others). Why is this?

With our human self-awareness and volition, we can shape our circumstances (to some extent). Yet we're significantly influenced by the environment in which we live, work and learn. The Myers-Briggs Type Indicator[9] personality test recognises this. The description for each profile contains the phrase:

> 'Sometimes life circumstances have not supported... the development and expression of their preferences.'

We overlook such factors whenever we say I (or they) *should have* known better or behaved more skilfully. Such declarations of judgement discourage reflection and reduce the possibilities for compassionate understanding. They also tend to place responsibility in a single place (me or them). Construing failure in someone or something takes less effort than asking: what might explain this?

So, what is failure? How do we perceive and calibrate it?

To me, failure is often contextual and highly dependent on beliefs, assumptions and ambitions. Perhaps I'm certain how things *should* be and *what is best* in a given situation. My convictions become expectations. When these aren't met, I call it failure, forgetting that I created the parameters in the first place.

Failure is often a product of the way I think. It's fruitless to want the world to be other than it is. When I catch myself pinning my hopes on a desire and making it a prediction, the only rational response is to laugh, or smile ruefully.

When other people are involved in a complex interplay of influences, intentions and dynamics, it can be harder to see my part in untoward or unwanted events. It helps if I recognise that all outcomes are *interesting* and worthy of examination. After all, in science, all results provide data, none is worthless.

This attitude fosters curiosity: why do things turn out the way they do? It creates space to explore, with imagination, the many factors that bring about unexpected, adverse or disappointing incidents. With perspective, I may accept my own errors or omissions, lessening any frustration, hurt or tendency to blame. Or perhaps I appreciate the restrictions or requirements placed on others, becoming more tolerant of actions that seem inexplicable or misguided.

In searching for greater understanding of the *seeds* of events, there is potential for learning and change. When I can't access the wherewithal for this search, I fall short in yet another way. However, to reproach myself would be like berating those raspberries… or the weather… or the moon!

Contemplations

- Choose a time that you judged yourself to have failed – what standards are you using to make this assessment? What factors and co-dependencies affected the outcome?
- What changes if you accept things as they are?

9 Perfect whole

Written in March 2015

One of my go-to books when I'm adrift is Parker Palmer's *Let Your Life Speak*.[16] I've read this book at least half a dozen times. And yet, when I picked it up recently, I read a passage that I hadn't knowingly seen before. In writing about the challenges of attempting to live in accordance with our own nature, with our unique combination of gifts and limitations, Palmer quoted author John Middleton Murry:

> *'For a good man to realise that it is better to be whole than to be good is to enter on a straight and narrow path compared to which his previous rectitude was flowery licence.'*

These words reminded me of a workshop for coaches, where I was one of a group of people invited to lead a session. The theme was 'Evolve, Coaching for the Future'.

The contributors had been chosen for their different experiences, approaches and styles. We hadn't been briefed, just invited to participate. We hadn't shared our sessions beforehand, and two of the three of us were completely unknown to each other. Yet, over the course of the day, it became clear that there was a single underlying message in all the sessions. We were each exploring how fear or anxiety limits what is possible – in a coaching client, in organisations, in ourselves as practitioners – and suggesting that the origins of caution lie in what is *un*known, *un*seen, *un*spoken, *un*acknowledged.

Clients and coaches are often not consciously aware of these '*uns*'. The sessions led by others explored the impact of such shadows in the context of mind and language, while I worked on a similar theme using the body. Using touch, we can surface our energetic survival patterns. We can also experience how it feels to recover our balance and be more centred.

In the workshop, each of the session leaders drew attention to the role of greater transparency in creating potential. The theme was that we become more *whole* if we can recognise, accept and include our foibles, doubts and confusions alongside our strengths, attributes and qualities. Each session leader used a different word or phrase to describe wholeness. However, I felt we were each calling forward a self of deep integrity, courage, clarity, intuition and compassion. In my language, this is the centred self, a still point in a maelstrom of being human.

Was the emerging theme a coincidence? For me, the subject of 'Evolve' catalysed a deeper order for the day, evoking an invitation to *organic* growth. This contrasts with a sense of *effort* in developing or learning. While both are about change, the spirit of evolving seems innate. It feels like a call to a *higher expression of self*, rather than a need to correct deficiencies or add new features.

From the day, one phrase remained with me: as coaches, our work is to be whole not perfect. Cognitively, I yelled an immediate 'yes' to this. Later, more reflectively and profoundly, I recalled that whole *is* perfect – that's the essential beauty of it.

While the workshop was for coaches, the need to be whole, rather than perfect, also relates to leadership. It seems to me that a tragedy of being human is that we *forget* we are already whole. In a unique and imperfect way, we're each perfect. In forgetting, we tie ourselves in knots trying to conceal or repair whatever we feel is lacking or tarnished.

It requires honesty, courage, humility and grace to reveal this essential humanness. It also requires discernment about how and when to honourably be transparent with others. It is indeed a path that makes being good look like flowery licence.

Contemplations

- How might you reveal a little more of your wholeness, be a little more transparent about both your wisdoms and warts? When you do this, what is the impact?

- What are the risks in being less certain, more fallible, less polished, more flawed? What will make it worthwhile to take those risks?

10 Dressing down
Written in August 2015

Recently, I've been on the receiving end of several adverse comments, reminding me of an incident from my first job. I had moved to London to work in a bank in the City. After initial training, I was placed in the treasury function, possibly because of my maths degree rather than a personal aptitude for financial trading. It was an alien world. Thankfully, kindly old hands helped me learn the ropes.

The details of the incident elude me now, though the emotional footprint remains. Broadly, I'd been asked to do some calculations for the boss and had made a mistake. His condemnation ended with: 'this means I can't trust *any* of your work'. That evening, being driven to the coast for the weekend, I sobbed the whole way. An error had been turned into a character defect – truly a 'dress down' Friday.

This tale reveals some flawed reasoning by my boss, escalating a single act to an 'always' or 'never' attribute. We all succumb to this kind of generalisation from time to time. Perhaps a single example of kindness *defines* a kind person, or a solitary discrepancy in a story makes the teller a liar. In making such inferences, we lose sight of someone's *wholeness*, which usually encompasses being *both* generous *and* mean, *both* truthful *and* inaccurate.

The ambiguity and contradiction of *both/and* is human nature: I'm often considerate, yet sometimes not; mostly I'm candid, occasionally not. In overlooking the light and shade in each other, we simplify human complexities and inconsistencies. For example, we create an airbrushed positive image of someone and then feel disappointed when they don't live up to our (undisclosed) expectations. With greater awareness of such constructs, we may be more able to examine our assumptions when feeling frustration or dissatisfaction towards others. If we identify the filters through which we're judging someone's behaviour, we're more likely to set them aside.

When I find myself mentally dressing down a friend or associate, I draw on a Chinese parable, adapted from *The Te of Piglet*:[10]

A man dug a well beside a road. Grateful travellers welcomed the Wonderful Well. One night someone fell into the well and drowned. People avoided the Dangerous Well. Later, it transpired that the drowned man was a criminal, trying to evade capture. He met his end in the Justice-Dispensing Well. Same well. Different views.

This story reminds me to practise suspending judgement. When someone does something out of character, I wonder what caused this departure. Reconnecting to their many qualities, I see them more clearly and compassionately. Often, I realise I've misinterpreted their actions, or credited them with imaginary superpowers. I am then able to engage more positively with whatever has occurred.

I also draw on the wisdom of this parable when I feel maligned. When dubbed rude, boring, selfish or aloof (to name but a few), the story of the well reminds me that I've also been called respectful, pioneering, generous and warm.

Same Amanda. Different views. All partial.

This is not to excuse occasions when I *have* been combative, thoughtless or arrogant (to name a few more). At these times the parable prompts me to explore the substance of the charges put to me. When I have been unskilful, it helps me recall that I can also be conciliatory, thoughtful or modest.

Balancing the *both/and* of human nature, I'm better able to discern whether a dressing down is warranted. If it is, I accept with grace and learn, whilst noting that it may not be a defining defect. If it's not, I'm learning to accept... and smile.

Contemplations

- When you feel criticised or judged, how might you avoid the extremes of dismissing the feedback or being crushed by it? How do you discern what's relevant and of value?

- When you feel disappointed in, or frustrated with, others, how might you gain insight into their situation?

 Energetic cheques

Written in October 2014

In the movie *Top Gun*, Tom Cruise's character, Maverick, is berated by his superior with the words:

'Your ego is writing cheques your body can't cash.'

This succinctly conveys a perennial difficulty in the way that many of us navigate the world. What I can *imagine immediately* greatly outstrips what I can *quickly achieve*. Put simply, I can easily envisage being at the top of a mountain – and overlook the reality of getting there. My mind can make plans that I'm not (yet) energetically equipped to fulfil.

In a plugged-in world, 'bandwidth' is a familiar term. Broadly, it's the maximum capacity for throughput in a digital communication path. We've experienced the delays or distortions of insufficient bandwidth. A movie hangs. A download takes forever. We become irritated or frustrated.

Now consider the possibility that, as a leader, you have an energetic bandwidth – a maximum capacity for throughput. In the flow of energy that comprises a life, some activities are energising and replenish or increase our capacity. Others deplete our reserves. When outflow exceeds inflow over time, we become overdrawn. This shows up physically as stress, agitation, hyperactivity or exhaustion. We become less efficient, less effective. Our wellbeing declines. Sometimes an illness or injury develops.

Yet, when organising my schedule, I don't often consider whether I have the *energetic resources* for the time commitments I'm making.

Paradoxically, pressure on our energetic bandwidth is often most acute at moments of great achievement. As an executive coach, I've supported a number of leaders through the recruitment process for their dream job. Since the outcome is outside our control, we work through the impact of being unsuccessful. However, I also guide clients to prepare for the effects of success.

Actually getting the job can be the more challenging option. Endorsed as the best candidate, the cheques my client wrote in thoughts and words will now be cashed energetically. They have to deliver, whilst being unproven. There are new relationships to establish, or existing ones to re-set. Demands on their time and energy escalate immediately – everyone wants a piece of the new boss. Energetic cheques may begin to bounce.

The living reality of success is materially different to the dream. This may come as a shock. The imagined future was founded on a partial, aspirational picture. Reality is an incoming flood of new information which tests processing capacity and stretches *cognitive* bandwidth. Less obviously, the nervous system is on alert for potential dangers in an unfamiliar setting. It's intense – and human emotions and physiology adjust more slowly to new circumstances than human minds.

Similar experiences occur whenever there is a material change in our work or life. If our response is to try to impose mind over matter and push through, we further increase pressure on a human system already at capacity. In the short term, this may be tolerable, but it quickly becomes unsustainable. Eventually, the body begins to creak around the edges. Most of us have been there.

To conduct ourselves more skilfully at an energetic level, we need to be realistic about our energetic bandwidth. What is our capacity? What supports us to maintain it? What clogs it up?

With clarity we can make wiser choices about the expectations we place *on ourselves* and avoid writing further dodgy cheques.

Contemplations

- Consider your bandwidth as a leader – what happens when your workload exceeds your current capacity for throughput? How might you support yourself to bring better balance to this energetic bank account?

- When you next squeeze an appointment into your schedule, what will support you to pause and ask: can I cash this energetic cheque?

12 System upgrades
Written in January 2015

I began this year in retreat, solitary and silent. It was a period of much needed self-examination and reflection. In the preceding months, I'd become increasingly ragged. My ability to be present was reduced, impacting the quality of my work. I was crabby and short-tempered with those I love. I was out of sorts and had lost contact with my essential nature, the inner compass that guides me to do my best work.

The erosion of my capacity was attributable to a gradual accumulation of causes, some self-inflicted. Others, such as frustrating IT, began as external events: Microsoft withdrew support for Windows XP, my printer broke, the new one had compatibility problems and I received catastrophic 'unhelp' from a helpdesk. These issues were exacerbated by my shortcomings: I was attached to keeping the familiar and was unable to make good decisions in order to move forward.

As December approached, my computer and I both needed attention! Even without adverse events, a computer eventually reaches a point where adding another program or app slows the system down. For a while, minor incompatibilities and inefficiencies can be managed by patches, reinstalls, clean-up tools or defragmenting the disk. Ultimately, more drastic action is required: upgrading the operating system.

In human terms, I feel a similar process applies. As we add tools, experience, knowledge and other apps to our repertoire, the incremental additions create little dissonances with our existing approaches.

As with technology, small internal conflicts can be handled for a time – through holidays, absorbing interests and other mental breaks that reconnect us with what matters. However, at some stage the inconsistencies begin to leak into our interactions with others, signalling the time for more fundamental change: an upgrade of our human operating system.

Self-leadership

Beneath what we do and say, we have a personal architecture of beliefs, values, principles and attitudes that characterises our leadership presence and practice. These inner structures shape our impact in the outer world. When their coherence is disturbed by new experiences or by development, it affects everything we do.

When this operating system becomes so sluggish and erratic that we have to work increasingly hard not to mess up, it's time to do the kind of inner work that Parker Palmer describes in *Let Your Life Speak*.[16] This was the place I'd reached by the end of last year.

First though, I had to deal with my computer. For a non-techie, installing a new operating system takes time and fortitude. I'm faced with options I don't fully understand, such as 'partition the hard disk?', which means I put a finger in the air and move on to reinstalling software and devices (some of which don't work) and configuring stuff. It's tiresome, exacting, frustrating. And I can only *hope* the result will be an improvement.

If that was daunting, setting out to reconfigure my human operating system was even more so! There are many ways of approaching inner work – my chosen path was a Buddhist retreat of meditation, study and reflection. It was tough, moving, humbling and profound. Somehow, in the discipline, a sense of integrity and peace unfolded, preparing me to approach a new year with some clarity. Although, of course, I am encountering compatibility issues as I readjust to life and work.

Contemplations

- When you are working at capacity for sustained periods of time, what begins to give? How might you monitor the coherence and health of your leadership practice?
- When you need to reconfigure your human operating system, how will you address this? What will motivate you to invest the time, energy and money required?

13 Letter from Falkland
Written in October 2015

For many years, I've lived in the Fife village of Falkland, which is steeped in history, with an old palace at its heart. The village is also home to a centre for leading-edge thinking and practice in stewardship, in the sense of taking care of place and people so that their potentials may be realised.

For me, the spirit of stewardship connects to my practice as a coach, dialogue practitioner, leader and human being. When I need to reflect on the complexities I face in challenging client situations, walking in the local landscape supports me. I particularly love climbing the nearby hill.

On maps, this hill is called East Lomond, although it is known locally as Falkland Hill. With its slightly higher companion, West Lomond, it is visible from Edinburgh and from some surprising places like the summit of Lochnagar in Deeside.

A circular walk from the village takes around two hours. It is both incredibly familiar and always different. Sometimes clouds shroud the domed top, or perhaps it's covered in snow, or so windy I can barely stand. The quality of light changes too, depending on the season and the weather.

My route starts in the village, taking me past the old factory and up through steep woodland. After twenty minutes, I rise above the trees and walk along the eastern shoulder. There is now much to see, from the fertile farmlands of Fife and the low hills that line the banks of the River Tay to the distant Grampian Mountains. If I turn to look behind me, the North Sea shimmers beyond St Andrews. After the sharp climb, my breathing now begins to ease. I feel the elements on my face and in my hair, and my mind begins to roam lightly through the knotty issues in my work or life.

A little later, I tackle the unforgiving haul to the summit, taking short stops to catch my breath. Alongside the physical effort, I rage at the difficulties I'm experiencing and blow them into the ground with each hard outbreath. While punishing, this final climb only takes a dozen minutes; and as I reach a grassy plateau and the stumpy pillar that marks the summit, horizons open all around me. The effect is stunning. My spirit soars and I pause to enjoy the moment.

The sense of spaciousness liberates me from my troubles.

Then, as I begin the descent, I give my complete attention to the path, which is precipitous, irregular and eroded. To place my feet carefully and maintain my balance, I need to be fully present. This brief respite from reflecting seems to allow my mind to find the crux of whatever I need to consider, reframe or probe.

These processes begin as the gradient lessens. On a broad grassy track, my body and mind slip into a gentle rhythm with a sense of joy: the hard work has been done! This *ease* invariably generates new insights.

The very nature of the hill seems to hold me to account – it is constant, grounded, steadfast and present. It seems that this reckoning is also an aspect of stewardship: I examine my practice with the intention of serving a wider system, of doing the right thing for both me and others.

Such stewardship of my practice is one strand of the discipline of professional supervision. The other two are: learning from both good and challenging moments in my work; and creating space to replenish my energy and nourish my ability to be present in adversity. Climbing Falkland Hill supports me in all three processes, helping me remain fit-for-practice.

The hill itself becomes my supervisor.

Contemplations

- What helps you to reflect on your leadership practice? How do you hold yourself to account?
- What nourishes and resources you, and supports you to keep doing your best work?

Leadership in conversations

Most leadership is enacted through the medium of conversation – whether meetings, presentations or one-to-ones. Attending to the shape and quality of our conversations and ensuring they are fit for purpose is an essential leadership task. We need to pay attention to the 'how' of our conversations, as well as the 'what', so that we can create the conditions for conversations to go well. This section explores such matters.

Beyond words

Handing over

Energy rising

The grittiness of dialogue

Gravitational pull

Holding conversations

Voice recognition

Beyond belief

Attention!

Naked truth

Sounds of silence

Conversation operating systems

Letter from Assynt

14 Beyond words
Written in August 2016

Back in the day, I was a director of finance in the NHS. Long before I encountered dialogue practices, my deputy and I were preparing for an important meeting that she'd called. We had to gain support from a local peer group for a crucial development. We were expecting opposition. My colleague was very clear and animated about how to push our agenda through.

Sensing potential for stalemate, I encouraged her to consider drawing out some of the objections early in the meeting, so she could respond to them along the way. She likened my suggestion to sprinkling food on the surface of a fish pond, so that fish rise and nibble. She added, wryly: 'you mean I should avoid my usual strategy of throwing in a stick of dynamite and collecting dead fish from the banks?'

We laughed at the time and still chuckle about it. It was a potent conversation. Her evocative image clarified my sense that some ways of dealing with resistance simply escalate it and result in casualties. Learning to engage with dissent more intentionally was one of the things that led me to the field of dialogue.

Over time, consciously embodying good practice in leadership conversations has become the backbone of my work. If I have clear intentions about the shape and quality of my contribution to a conversation, I'll be more effective. It's also crucial to cultivate capacity to handle myself well in gritty situations.

When I introduce dialogue as a particular conversational form, I begin by distinguishing it from debate and discussion. In drawing attention to words that are often used interchangeably, I invite people to explore their sense of the purpose and tone of these different types of conversation

To nurture this interest, I describe two kinds of contribution to conversations:

- Advocacy: stating my position or view, making a point; and

- Inquiry: drawing out what I don't yet know or understand.

We can use these terms to describe and better understand the shape of a conversation. For example, debate is an exchange of advocacy, arguing for and against a proposal, while dialogue balances advocacy and inquiry.

With this light framework, we can observe the architecture of conversations and begin to examine whether they're fit for purpose. We may also get an inkling of what to modify to positively influence the tenor of an exchange.

The 'fish pond' example gives a flavour of this. Rather than increase the intensity of her advocacy in response to expected challenges, my colleague added some inquiry, drawing out the legitimate concerns of others. In changing the shape of her contribution, she changed the shape of the conversation. As a result, she was able to outline her agenda in a way that showed she understood the disquiet that her colleagues were feeling. She adjusted some details, and obtained agreement for her direction of travel.

Changing the shape of a contribution or conversation is not enough. We can say the same words with different impact, depending on factors such as tone, pace, posture and presence. When business-critical conversations become highly charged, we're likely to be tense and off-balance, operating from fight, flight or freeze. Physiology is in charge: we're focused on short-term survival, not creativity, collaboration or long-term effectiveness.

To optimise the impact of what we say, we also need to attend to the energetic quality of what we say. This means we need to be able to positively adjust our energy and physiology by using something like a centring process. Beyond words, this plays a significant part in determining our impact.

Contemplations

- Choose a conversation you regularly participate in: what do you notice about the shape and energy of it?
- How might you contribute differently, in the shape of what you say and/or the energy you bring to it?

15 Handing over
Written in September 2014

Watching the British sprint relay teams at the European Championships last month, I was inspired. Their performance was fabulous, of course, but even more stirring was their camaraderie, cohesion and sense of supporting each other in a shared endeavour. Their success is a sharp contrast to the woes of a few years ago, when British teams seemed unable to get the baton to the finish line.

Back then, I was immersed in a learning review of a project in serious difficulties. I spent time with the people involved, getting their different perspectives on what had occurred, and wrote up a synthesis of their experiences. To harvest the learning, I used the metaphor of a relay team, quoting the former sprinter Michael Johnson who, at the Beijing Olympics, said 'the point of the relay is to get the baton to the end of the race'. The US men's team had dropped the baton and, later, the British team was disqualified because one of their handovers wasn't within the rules.

Basically, it doesn't matter how talented or fast each relay athlete is if they don't pass the baton cleanly between them. When an individual runner has the baton, they can concentrate on their own technique, speed, expertise and execution. However, at handovers, to pass the baton successfully, two people need to co-operate, co-ordinating their intent, pace and actions in a confined space.

Three short moments of exchange constitute the greatest risk to their collective aim.

In the case of the troubled project, the learning review revealed that the critical nature of handovers hadn't been recognised. Each person was focused on doing their own part well – but for itself, rather than as a piece of the whole. At the human interfaces, where responsibilities were transferred from one person (or team) to another, important information was lost.

This isn't unusual. In organisations, the risks associated with handovers are often managed with checklists and procedures. However, this tends to capture only explicit knowledge. Another kind of knowledge – the stuff of experience, instinct, mindset and taken-for-granted assumptions – is mostly out of consciousness. Such tacit knowledge is easy to overlook and is most likely to come to light through conversation.

Even when the risks are understood, handover conversations are often not fit for purpose. When a baton gets dropped, we tend to attribute fault to others. We don't think of the shape and quality of our conversations as a contributory factor. Yet they often are, in guises such as our unspoken beliefs about the *relationship* between talk and action.

In *The World Café*,[11] the authors distinguish between a *traditional view*, in which this relationship is linear – talk leads to action – and an *emerging view*, in which conversation is a 'core process'. In the latter, conversation *is* action, rather than something to be got out of the way so we can get to the real stuff. In this view, stakeholders in an issue talk together to share perspectives and insights about their situation; to plan and test responses; and to observe, reflect and continually update the way the issue is framed. An ongoing conversation creates the conditions for responding to changing circumstances, in which there may be multiple interfaces where batons need to change hands.

At these interfaces, as we hand over a baton, we need to co-ordinate our intention, pacing and actions with those of others to get our combined efforts safely to the finish line. This requires that we identify the risks involved and create the conditions for the kind of conversation that will get the baton safely handed over.

Contemplations

- What does this metaphor evoke in you?
- Where might you, or someone in your team or system, be at risk of dropping a baton when transferring a remit or job to others? What is at stake? How might you improve the quality of the handover?

16 Energy rising
Written in December 2015

As an executive coach, I support my clients to *study* themselves in their interactions with others and the world and to identify how they react in pressured or stressful situations. Most reactivity is rooted in our 'fight/flight/freeze' system and is primarily physiological. Under duress, cognitive understanding is not sufficient to change our behaviour. However, in using embodied approaches, we can explore our reactions physically and apply an antidote, a centring practice that enables us to recover poise and effectiveness.

While I love doing this work with clients, I also use embodied practices myself to good effect. With regular centring practice, I've become more able to be present, resourceful and skilful in a variety of situations, particularly when the going gets tough. When I'm experiencing the discomfort of criticism, confrontation or disagreement, I'm more able to remain engaged. After all, if I can't *stay in* a charged conversation, I have no *influence* over its outcome.

Engaging in the martial art of T'ai Chi Ch'üan provides me with the clearest evidence of the consequences of being *unable* to stay in charged situations. I'm not a natural martial artist and, while I can be diligent in practising solo movement sequences, working with a partner on martial applications has always been a stretch. I'm often tempted to avoid this aspect of practice. This means I don't improve. And so I'm even more likely to duck out.

One thing I've come to understand *viscerally* is that even if we're adept at something individually, the energetic temperature rises when another person is involved. With additional energy in play, we can become less skilful – any individual competence is diluted by the complexity of engaging with someone else. Recognising this, I've used centring practices to change my focus to increasing my ability to handle the *intensity* of martial interactions rather than trying to be good at them. This helps me to stay in the practice and to learn.

In a conversation, the relationship between the number of people and the scale, intensity and complexity of the energetic dynamics that arise is not linear. This has implications for the way we handle ourselves.

The starting point is that when two people are talking, there is a relationship between them. There are three energies to navigate: two individuals and the dynamic they create between them.

Add a third person and there are three relationships to attend to. Add a fourth and the number of relationships increases to six, as each person relates to three others. So, in a conversation, rising from two people (one relationship) to four people (six relationships) doesn't double the energetic complexity, it more than triples it. If there are six people present, there are fifteen dynamics to consider.

At some point, the accumulating energies begin to overwhelm those present and affect their ability to handle themselves skilfully. The point at which this occurs depends on many personal factors and our capacity as an individual to handle the complex currents and tides that are in play. This way of looking at what unfolds in a group can help us to see when we are becoming ineffective, individually and together, so we can then take steps to regroup.

The energy in a room can be influenced by practical measures such as agendas or timetables, which help with containment. The way a room is set up also shapes an energetic footprint – a room arranged for a panel and audience creates a different space to a circle of chairs. Paying attention to these factors and developing personal capacity to stay cool and collected when energy is rising can all help a conversation stay on track.

Contemplations

- Pay attention to levels of energy in groups of different sizes and configurations. Which factors heighten energy? Which reduce it?

- Reflect on your own experiences in a variety of groups – under what circumstances do you feel at ease? At what threshold do you become uncomfortable and how does this affect your contribution?

17 The grittiness of dialogue

Written in February 2014

Recently, I discovered a way to describe the visceral experience of being in dialogue, eliminating a whole lot of conceptual explanation. The catalyst was a need to identify the essence of dialogue for a taster session in a leadership development programme. The concentrated nature of a short workshop sharpened my thinking – the experience of many years means I can overcomplicate matters!

I wanted to avoid two potential potholes:

- Too much presenting (or advocacy) in a context of dialogue, which balances advocacy and inquiry; and

- Giving an impression that dialogue is a form of sublime, Zen-like conversation.

I easily succumb to both these traps – but I'm conscious of the tendencies that lead me into the first and so can take avoiding action. In contrast, I often only realise I've fallen into idealising dialogue when others reflect back their understanding of what I've said. I aimed to use the imperative of designing this workshop session to more faithfully represent this type of conversation.

It is true that dialogue can have moments of great expansion and lucidity. However, it is usual to pass through some *earthier* territory before these arise. On this rougher ground, it's easy to lose heart, especially if we expected a smooth path. If I can better communicate the true nature of dialogue, I might support more people to navigate this tricky terrain.

In my quest to convey the look and feel of engaging in dialogue, with minimum presenting, I drew on Scharmer's 'Fields of Conversation'.[18] This framework describes the energetic experience of four distinct conversational paradigms, offering a language to distinguish between them.

Leadership in conversations

The first field recognises that many conversations have a *routine*, co-created and held in place by all involved. These routines are habitual and occur largely on autopilot. They serve some purposes well and others less well. When a different kind of conversation is required, it can be hard to escape the grip of established interactions. An attempt to move away from familiar patterns can lead to *grittiness* in the form of frustration, irritation, hostility, anxiety and other states of heightened energy. This is the flavour of the second field.

Navigating the grittiness of this unsettled and unsettling energy requires mindfulness and presence. If we are composed and able to welcome and accept different outlooks and concerns, a third kind of conversation evolves, in which opinions are less tightly held. This creates room for more curiosity about the views of others.

This third field represents a significant step towards dialogue. It might feel like calmer water after turbulent rapids, yet it can be complex, fast moving and intense: the issues matter; leaders are opinionated and expert in their domain; the pace is pressured. It's certainly not Zen-like. So, how can I evoke this in fewer words?

What I came up with is this: recall an occasion when you've been in a struggle with yourself about something that matters – you have a dilemma and you're digging deep for an answer. What do you experience as you do this?

And, if this is how it feels when you're trying to *settle your own mind* about a complex issue, imagine how it might feel to seek settlement *amongst many minds*. This may give you a real sense of what it means to be in dialogue.

Contemplations

- When does your familiarity with your terrain lead to less clarity for others, rather than more? How might you *distil* your experience to communicate potently?

- Recall a time when you've faced a dilemma and have had to dig deep for a resolution. What can you learn from this about the process of finding settlement amongst many minds?

18 Gravitational pull
Written in November 2012

During some case-work in a dialogue workshop, a participant was outlining their engagement in an intense and uncompromising exchange. In these sessions, we explore 'stuck' conversations with the aim of shedding light on them. We're not trying to resolve the presenting issue; we're aiming to reveal aspects of the conversation that are being overlooked by those involved. We use frameworks from dialogue practice to support this process.

Key to this is holding a sense of neutral curiosity, which is particularly important for me as I am leading the session. However, in this case, I got drawn in to the story, as if it had an irresistible gravitational pull. I lost perspective. What was going on?

The gist of the case was this:

- Two people with opposing positions were strongly arguing their case;
- Reputations were at stake; and
- Emotions were engaged.

The parties were relatively evenly matched: one had more position power, while the other held the power to deliver results (or not). There was a sense of stalemate – neither could disregard the other and impose their agenda. It's a common dynamic – two knowledgeable people, each increasingly wedded to their view. Convinced they are right, they dismiss or discount alternatives.

A key principle of dialogue practice is to regard each voice in a conversation as being of equal value and validity. In workshops we try to embody this. It's a delicate balance to support our colleague whilst being prepared to say 'I'm seeing this differently'. Mostly, we're able to maintain this. However, when we listen to a highly charged disagreement, it's human to take sides, to feel a gravitational pull towards one perspective. Yet, as we give one voice more credence, we are less able to value the other.

The purpose of holding perspective and appreciating the legitimacy of each voice is to explore impartially how each person shapes what unfolds. This opens the potential to hear an exchange in new ways, even for those enmeshed in it. Recognising both our own part in what transpires and the influence of existing patterns of conversation supports us to tackle similar situations skilfully.

In losing perspective on this occasion, I was less able to support the learning process for the group. It was an unsettling experience and a reminder that building capacity for holding steady in charged situations is an ongoing process. It was also food for thought: when it's possible to lose our centre and neutrality in a conflict in which we have no *direct* involvement, how much stronger is the gravitational pull when we have a stake in the outcome?

This story highlights the role of our demeanour and energy in situations where we need to navigate difference skilfully. Whilst using models and tools helps us to understand a conversational dynamic *cognitively*, it doesn't help us grasp what's happening at an energetic level. Knowledge doesn't help us keep our head when all about are losing theirs (to adapt the poet Rudyard Kipling). What does help is recovering our composure and presence.

We each have a threshold for remaining calm, open and creative in the midst of a charged situation. When we cross this threshold, we're likely to succumb to the gravitational pull of a narrative, narrowing our perspective. We favour one story over another and lose our bearings. If we notice this, we can take action to recover centre and regain perspective. Being able to respect each voice is a defining aspect of dialogue and makes it more likely that a conversation will be generative.

Contemplations

- How often in a day do you get drawn into one version of events while discounting another? What hooks you in? What is the impact?

- Recall a disturbing and charged exchange that you've witnessed. Where do your sympathies lie? If you regard all voices to be of equal value, what changes?

19 Holding conversations
Written in May 2015

The more dialogue-related work I do, the greater my appreciation for the connection between the *outcome* of a conversation and the *climate* within which it's held. What I mean by outcome is more than the immediate upshot – it includes how the conversation impacts relationships and the bigger system.

Climate is harder to articulate. It's a mash-up of ingredients, such as energetic feel; quality of engagement; levels of safety; rhythm and tone of voices; perceptions of power; and freedoms to speak. Very few of these are concrete and yet their combined effect is palpable. We might liken climate to a bowl, in which the usable space is defined by solid material such as china or wood. To create a fruitful space in which to talk and listen, we can explore how to use tangible factors, such as setting and conduct, to make a container.

The nature of a physical container determines what it can hold – a flimsy plastic dish distorts when filled with hot contents, for example. In a similar way, the fabric of a container for conversation influences the levels of intensity, turbulence and discomfort that can be safely handled by those present. A routine conversation may be sustained by social customs, a formal agenda and a chairperson, whilst a 'higher, deeper, wider' conversation (as one client describes dialogue) calls for more deliberate and nuanced holding.

For example, to nurture a climate that welcomes differences – which are often passionately promoted or doggedly defended – those present must collectively be able to accept and acknowledge irritation, frustration, dislike and other highly charged feelings. Together, they must also find the grace, compassion and humility to absorb self-doubt, embarrassment, disappointment and regret. Put simply, they must build capacity to *contain* whatever arises, however difficult, and continue to listen with respect and curiosity until there is a glimpse of shared insight into what really matters. This changes the quality of the conversation.

Leadership in conversations

In my view, every conversation has a container, whether or not we pay attention to its nature. When ignored, a container still shapes what unfolds, in the way the layout of a room may go unremarked yet may subtly enable or limit collaboration. To be sure we can talk about important issues with appropriate frankness and depth, we must take note of our container and consider whether it is resilient enough to support our aspirations.

For example, if we expressly attend to how we will *receive* what is said, we establish a shared willingness to recognise and consider each voice. This, in turn, encourages greater openness. The very act of turning towards such matters and bringing them into awareness fundamentally changes what is possible. In *Dialogue and the Art of Thinking Together*,[18] William Isaacs is unequivocal: 'no consciously held container, no dialogue.'

Explicitly exploring and articulating the shared conditions for *holding* a conversation enhances our collective capacity to engage with each other. Yet how much time do we typically invest in cultivating and maintaining this aspect of our conversations? I know I'm not alone in finding the magnetism of tasks, decisions and problem-solving hard to resist. The short-term attraction of content and achievement easily seduces me into skipping over the non-urgent business of creating a container.

When things are going well, this doesn't matter. If things get messy, it's too late – emotions are already running high, ambiguity and uncertainty abound and self-interest predominates. In the midst of all this, it's much harder to attend to *holding* the conversation. And so, in neglecting to ask what kind of space we intend to establish for our conversation, I create my own circumstances, time after time.

Contemplations

- Recall a difficult or unpleasant conversation – when you reflect on the conditions in which the conversation took place, what do you notice? What shaped the conversation, before a word was spoken?

- When you next approach an important conversation, how might you influence those present to engage in creating the climate for it?

20 Voice recognition
Written in May 2013

When we advocate, we speak for a position, explain a point of view or make a case for a course of action. Advocating is directional in nature and, when people around a table hold different views, it can feel like obstruction, resistance or criticism, especially when the stakes are high in terms of performance or reputation. Things can get lively and uncomfortable.

To handle difference constructively, we might draw on wisdom from dialogue, a form of conversation that William Isaacs[18] describes as:

> '...a way of taking the energy of our differences and channeling it toward something that has never been created before.'

Respecting is a dialogue practice that supports us to be skilful when dealing with opposing ideas. To harness the energy of difference requires that we acknowledge and respect the *legitimacy* of other perspectives.

In dialogue, each view is held to be valid in the context of the knowledge, experience and understanding of the speaker. If I'm able to receive the opinions of others and hold them in parity with my own voice, I contribute to fostering a climate in which deeper, more personal truths may be spoken from the heart or soul. I become a witness to the rich variety of ways in which people make sense of the world. New possibilities germinate in the fertile soil of many truths.

In practising respect and recognising the value of all voices, we create the potential for difference to be generative rather than awkward, inconvenient, confrontational or irritating. When we fall short in respecting, we tend to discount or dismiss the views of others. We might try to persuade them to see the error of their ways. Or we might ignore differences and carry on as if everyone is in agreement.

Fostering the creative energy of diverse views also entails respecting our own contribution, our own voice. When we're unsure of ourselves, or uncertain how dissent will land, we can decide that the effort of speaking out is too great. Instead, we dilute or withhold our voice and a conversation is impoverished.

Respecting is about voice recognition: hearing, acknowledging and appreciating varied expressions of human experience, without necessarily agreeing with them. If we don't respect different voices, we miss the opportunity to explore them. We lose potential for stimulation, creative spark, expansive thinking and making connections. In understanding more deeply *how and why* people see things as they do, new thinking may unfold.

With so much at stake, why is it so challenging to *practise* respecting?

Intellectually, it's easy to accept that all ideas have value and that diversity and dissent enrich a conversation by offering opportunities for fresh insights. However, for many of us, difference is linked with discord or even conflict. It comes with an unsettling energy, strongly associated with exclusion, approbation, self-consciousness or stress. It's a tall order to practise respect when we feel isolated, wrong, wronged, angry or anxious. To do so, we need to recover our composure and centre.

To centre, we hold ourselves well, aligning our posture. We bring attention to the sensation of breathing and perhaps softly count our breaths (or simply count to ten). In charged, pressured or uncomfortable circumstances, this helps us to regain presence and equanimity. Then we can re-engage with others with greater respect.

Contemplations

- How do you handle difference? What is your underlying belief about it – do you see it as problematic or productive?
- Are you inclined to have too much or too little respect for the views of others? What is the impact in your conversations? How might you practise holding all views in equal respect?

21 Beyond belief
Written in June 2013

In conversations, inquiring energy invites participation, awareness and potential. It brings a sense of opening. When we inquire, we seek out what is not yet known or understood, such as new data, or a deeper appreciation of how others have formed their view. The dialogue practice of *suspending judgement* supports this by encouraging curiosity about the provenance, relevance and validity of what's being said.

Suspending judgement starts within. In our *internal dialogue,* we notice our judgements and opinions and set them aside *for a moment.* If I'm sure I'm right, this means considering that I may be wrong. This very possibility creates room in my mind (and heart) for different perspectives and opportunities. If I then invite others to loosen their attachment to *their* preferred way forward, we may enrich the quality of our collective thinking and decisions.

Making judgements is a natural and largely helpful human process and suspending judgement doesn't mean being non-judgemental. Instead, it is the practice of noticing our judgements and paying attention to how they colour our thinking and limit what's possible. Assigning value allows us to make choices. However, each time we adopt one path, we exclude others.

We often make (and hold) judgements about people and their motivations on the flimsiest of data. Perhaps we ascribe a deliberate desire to be difficult to someone who opposes our position. We overlook the possibility that they have an alternative interpretation of an issue because their knowledge, interests, and emotional and cognitive reference points are uniquely theirs. In suspending our own certainties, we may be more able to recognise this.

And so, when a client expresses disbelief and annoyance about the actions of a colleague, I often joke that (despite appearances) people are usually in leadership roles because of their attributes. Together, we reflect how the colleague might have put together their reasoning and what might be influencing them. This requires humility, but may generate insight into why the colleague is going about things in a particular way.

In suspending judgement, we do *not* change our mind. Instead, we acknowledge that it's unlikely that we have *all* the relevant information, experience or insights. We notice the impact of our mindset on our capacity for creative thinking. Then we put the mindset aside for a moment and look at a situation anew, without overlaying it with what we already 'know'. We ask: *what if… this doesn't hold true?*

Any intention to suspend judgement is up against a human predisposition that is deeply rooted. It can also be counter to our training and personal preferences. As leaders, we're *paid* to make judgements – and to make them quickly, confidently, decisively. More generally, at school, in the workplace and in life, we've typically been rewarded for 'answers' and certainty. It requires effort to *'not know'*, even for a moment. Countering such an ingrained habit of thinking requires commitment.

The poet Rumi evokes an ideal:

> 'Out beyond ideas of wrong-doing or right-doing there is a field. I'll meet you there.'

When we're able to suspend judgement, we move beyond polarity in our thinking: this not that, either/or, right/wrong. This fosters a different kind of conversation, in which we speak of *a* truth, rather than *the* truth. When there are many truths, there are few certainties, and this creates the potential for seeing things afresh.

Contemplations

- Choose an issue where you are firmly affiliated to a particular point of view – in what ways does this limit your outlook?
- When a colleague next opposes your view, how might you ascertain how you've come to different judgements?

22 Attention!
Written in July 2013

Listening, or attending, is one of four *dialogue practices* outlined by Garrett, Isaacs and others.[2] It is an act of receiving, and to engage in dialogue is to invite *reciprocity* in listening, in the acts of receiving and being received. We give our attention openly, inclusively, to others, whether we agree with them or not. We build our capacity for accepting the human experience of others. In this way, the practice of listening holds potential for change. When we truly hear what someone says, we release them from repeating their message.

How can we hone our listening practice?

To me, it's about being mindful of both the *whereabouts* and *intensity* of our listening attention.

In terms of whereabouts, we can become increasingly aware of whether we are staying with what another person is saying, or getting caught up in what we might say in response.

We can also become more conscious of *what* we're paying attention to and with what *intent*. Perhaps we're listening to a story, an explanation, a proposal, an hypothesis, in order to assess if we agree or not. Perhaps we're listening for information, facts or ideas, in order to support or refute a view. These kinds of listening focus on the *content* of what is being said. When we truly receive another person's perspective, we listen *beyond* their narrative. We acknowledge the emotional and energetic expression of a fellow human being.

In terms of intensity of attention, we might consider the impact of listening too keenly or too loosely. Voices can be tentative or fragile. It can take courage to speak, particularly about something deeply personal.

To calibrate the intensity of listening, we might imagine that voices are made of fine glass: if we grip the glass too hard, it may shatter; if we grip it too lightly, it may fall and smash. We hold glass carefully, polishing it to clear its surface of smears and smudges, so we can look through and see the world beyond. If we were able to extend this delicate care to the voices of others and to our internal voice, what would we experience?

When I'm rocked by unpleasant news, or when I'm trying to articulate something that really matters to me, I want those around me to be still, listening. I want to be met, accompanied. It requires a serenity of spirit to receive great pain, anger, sadness or anxiety with equanimity, in contrast with the popular notion of active listening. When someone is able to listen to me in this way, I feel truly held and acknowledged.

And so I actively work on developing and refining my ability to listen to all that is hard to hear. I'm inspired in this by Oriah Mountain Dreamer. In her poem *The Invitation*,[4] she evokes the courage needed for skilful listening and says:

> *'I want to know if you will stand in the centre of the fire with me and not shrink back.'*

This call to attention relates to our inner dialogue as well as to conversations with others. We shy away from our less palatable thoughts and our uncomfortable feelings, crowding them out with tasks and the many demands we place on ourselves. If we do not listen to our own difficult experiences, how can we listen to those of others?

It requires huge resolve to stand in this kind of fire and not recoil from the many uncomfortable truths of being human. And yet, if we practise with ourselves, we may find we have more steadfastness to receive others.

Contemplations

- To what extent are you able to stand in the fire with yourself and truly accept the parts you would rather ignore or disown?

- What do you tend to listen *for*? What will motivate you to more often listen beyond words?

23 Naked truth
Written in April 2013

In unsettling times, I often find solace and inspiration in the countryside around the village where I live. Recently, in one week of dawn walks, I watched an insouciant fox, locked gazes with a deer, witnessed a woodpecker beat out its spring message and stood beneath a waterfall as early rays of sunlight sparkled through icicles as thick as my arm. In the rhythm of walking and breathing, I reaffirm my sense of life, of being part of a vibrant tapestry.

These walks took place in a week that I cancelled a leadership retreat that I'd been organising because it had failed to attract participants. I was tempted to keep the cancellation quiet: when I let people down, I fear my reputation will be tarnished, or that I'll be seen as unsuccessful, unreliable or worse.

Instead, I chose to be open, even though something I held dear hadn't generated a resounding response in others. My transparency was prompted by the dialogue practice of *authentic voice*, or speaking mindfully from a place of deeper personal truth, regardless of how it might be received by others.

Authentic voice is about putting more of myself into a conversation. I don't second-guess what others might think or feel, which might tempt me to adapt, edit or embellish my words in the hope of a soft landing. I don't try to protect myself from imagined judgements or adverse reactions. Instead, I choose to disclose that something in which I invested time, energy and money has not borne fruit. I try to admit my disappointment without making it a burden for others.

The truth is an acquired taste. Authenticity can be raw, intense, naked. It reveals what we often cover up: emotions, uncertainty and human frailty. If we're unused to expressing our *real* thinking, our feelings or our deeper sense of a situation, our authentic voice may be rusty. We may then become self-conscious when we express it. Similarly, if we're unused to hearing this kind of candour, we may experience the kind of discomfort we'd feel if a colleague undressed in front of us.

In my case, the main impediment to speaking frankly is fear of tarnishing an important relationship. Yet, if I can find the courage to be open and genuine and make more of myself available to others, it may free others to acknowledge their own concerns. While being more honest can be testing in the short term, in the longer term a relationship may be strengthened. In contrast, if I withhold my truth, I am signalling that I don't trust myself and/or others to bear the weight of it.

To generate the fortitude to speak truly, I draw inspiration from part of *The Invitation*[4] by Oriah Mountain Dreamer:

> *'I want to know if you can disappoint another to be true to yourself.*
> *If you can bear the accusation of betrayal and not betray your own soul.'*

This is an uncomfortable demand for integrity. If I'm prepared to renounce my truth for the approval of others, what else might I dishonour or disown? If I'm prepared to sever my connection with my very essence, what value will others place on my connections with them?

In practising authentic voice, we deepen our contact with others through acknowledging our shared humanness. In an uncertain and complex world, we need this quality in our leadership conversations. If we are disloyal to our very nature, what is the worth of our loyalty to others?

Contemplations

- In what circumstances do you modify what you say to try and mitigate discomfort, conflict, worry or embarrassment? What underlies this?
- How might you bring more of yourself into your conversations? How might you grow capacity to receive the unsettling or unwelcome truths of others?

24 Sounds of silence

Written in February 2015

Since returning from a silent retreat, I find myself talking a lot about not talking. The irony doesn't escape me. While words can't fully express the experience and impact of silence, I continue to explore how I might articulate its merit in conversations.

I've written about silence before – in my book, *Pause for Breath*,[2] and in an article for *Coaching at Work* magazine (see page 92). The latter describes silence as part of the landscape – a textural backdrop into which sounds seem to fall and dissolve.

In *Pause for Breath*,[2] I consider 'making silence' as an active contribution to conversations. To be skilful with silence, it helps to acclimatise to its unsettling nature. If we make peace with our own *disquiet*, we can be more at ease with any awkwardness that arises in others.

When introducing dialogue practices to others, I invite them to notice silences, by invoking words attributed to the classical composer Claude Debussy:

'Music is the spaces between the notes.'

I take this to mean that musical spaces, apparently empty, have tone, timbre and other qualities associated with sound. In conversation, if silent interludes in the rhythm of our verbal exchanges feel uneasy or prickly – and they often do – this may give an indication of the 'music' of the talk.

If we can learn to discern it, silence yields potent information about the energetic mood of a conversation. By paying attention to absences of sound and being curious about their nature, we begin to distinguish between one silence and another. We come to recognise their nuances. Some are tense or anxious, others thoughtful or fertile. Some signal beginnings, others completion. Some represent acceptance or intimacy, others dissent or distance. In noticing, we gradually build a lexicon for the moments when words cease.

When silence occurs, it's often arresting. Its very unexpectedness can bring a feeling of exposure, as if we've come to a cliff edge. We're confronted by a precipitous space. Suddenly self-conscious, there may be a rush to fill the void with humour or soothing remarks, or an attempt to *a-void* it with an abrupt change of topic. In these defensive routines, valuable opportunities for deeper connection are lost.

If, instead, we can become accustomed to the disquiet of silence, we may more actively be able to embrace it and participate in it. Shared silence grants a pause, a moment when there's nothing to listen to and we don't need to speak. In this brief respite, we can turn our attention inward and take proper account of what we're thinking and feeling in response to what's been said. In reaching for a *deeper truth* within ourselves, we enrich what we eventually say, to collective benefit.

The music of this deeper truth (the dialogue practice of authentic voice) is composed in the silences of our internal dialogue. Like their external counterparts, such silences come in a range of forms and textures and are easy to ignore, lightly dismiss or resolutely paper over. And yet, if we attend to them and rest in their subtleties, we hear more clearly the harmonies and dissonances in the notes of our inner voices.

Listening to the music within, imagine what we might say?

Contemplations

- Notice your response to silences in conversations – what happens within? Do you want to withdraw, or interject? How does this vary with the tone and context of the silence?

- How might you build a lexicon for different kinds of collective silence? How might you support yourself and others to remain in the spaces between words?

25 Conversation operating systems

Written in September 2017

I am exploring how to better explain my dialogue-related work, which draws attention to the relationship between the shape and quality of conversations and what happens next. Some forms of conversation are more useful for particular purposes than others. Therefore, to create conditions that support the conversation we want to have, it pays to understand the influences at play.

This often means consciously changing the way we handle ourselves and engage with others, which can present a stumbling block for leaders, who tend to be adept at 'good enough' conversations. Decades of experience in talking and listening, coupled with a successful career, can create a blind spot about our proficiency. And when our conversations don't turn out well, it's easy to attribute this to the shortcomings of others.

In my search for a narrative, I'm road-testing a software metaphor. In 'System upgrades' (see page 36), I liken the process of leadership development to adding software and apps to a device. When we add to our repertoire in a piecemeal way, our ability to enact a new approach will depend on our disposition and beliefs, our internal operating system, if you like. For example, it may be difficult to learn to give appreciative feedback if our underlying attitude is to be critical.

What is the parallel for teams and organisations?

In a working alliance of several people, individual energies and tendencies combine to configure a collective operating system, a received way of going about things. While this patterning may be influenced by factors such as an organisation's purpose, customs, practices and culture, it becomes *tangible* in the way people talk and listen to each other. The look and feel of human interactions is an underlying code for communication – a conversation 'operating system' which, without attention, endures as people come and go.

In technology, an OS runs largely in the background. However, it determines whether or not programs and apps will work. Similarly, a conversation OS will favour some types of exchange and be incompatible with others. For instance, code that emphasises results and competition may limit the scope for talking about collaboration or innovation.

Making this connection, it's clear why some crucial conversations get derailed. If fruitless patterns recur, frustration sets in, especially if new tools or techniques don't deliver. Upgrading the OS requires something radical: collectively putting in the work to understand how conversations take shape and to develop new human 'software' that enables rich and rewarding conversations.

This involves team members learning to pay attention to the 'how' of a conversation as well as the 'what'. When we prepare for an important conversation, most of us think about the outcome we want and the things we'll say to get that result. We tend to give less consideration to the environment (operating system), which may be enabling unhelpful conversational 'apps' to run, such as repetitive point-scoring between A and B, habitual resistance from C, routine discounting of D, and collective avoidance of perennially difficult issues and tolerance of misused power.

If, instead, a team wants to create an environment in which they are able to speak frankly, they need to cultivate the practice of listening attentively and with curiosity and respect. To do this, it is helpful to talk about the conduct that will foster such a climate. When behaviour diverges from these aspirations, it will require presence of mind and courage to draw attention to this and get back on track. So it is also important to ask: how will we hold ourselves to account?

Contemplations

- How might you describe the conversation operating system for a team you are part of?
- What coding is running in the background and how does this shape what plays out?

26 Letter from Assynt
Written in May 2016

Assynt, in the far north west of Scotland, is a place where time is made visible. Comprising some of the oldest rocks in Europe, laid bare by the elements, the geology of this area raised questions that led to the theories of continental drift and plate tectonics. Based on observations of this landscape, geologists posited, for the first time, that the ground beneath our feet isn't simply a sequential layering. Instead, it's created by complex currents of molten rock deep beneath us, and by turbulent clashes nearer the surface that crush, separate, upend and fold the Earth's crust.

Over millions of years, landscapes we take as *given* alter in shape and location: we live in an almost inconceivable process of continuing change that is completely outside our influence. Sometimes, of course, we witness the drama of the shifting ground – a house on a cliff falls into the sea, a sink hole appears and swallows a field, or an earthquake rattles a bridge to destruction.

As if this isn't enough, the elements curate the landscape through erosion, flow, pooling, sandblasting, freezing and other processes.

Everything we see as stable is a product of instability. Here in Assynt, a beautiful sloping cove of sheltered pasture is the sunken roof of a cave, where cliffs have been excavated by the sea. Elsewhere, beneath the grandeur of a steep mountain, lies a graveyard of fallen stone, shattered by ice. Further afield, marine fossils on the summit of Everest demonstrate that it was once at sea level.

And so, a belief in an unchanging landscape is foolhardy, in the long run.

Similarly, though on a different scale, a belief in an unchanging self is also unwise. Over a lifetime, we hold different things to be important at different times. Our perspective changes, not least as we inhabit a variety of primary identities: child, student, employee, partner, carer… to name but a few.

Despite this shifting ground, many of us believe the landscape of 'self' has substance and is enduring. We talk of knowing ourselves and having strong principles or values. Yet I find that wherever I solidify my view about what is right or wrong, good or bad, possible or not, I become quick to judge and susceptible to being judged.

In adhering to a particular identity, I am on precarious terrain. For example, I see myself as a disciplined person and regard this as important. So, when someone called me undisciplined, I felt it keenly. The truth is that I do sometimes lack discipline and am not proud of this. And so the accusation ruptured the crust I've formed around me and shook me. For a while I struggled with two conflicting versions of myself and felt slightly broken.

In acknowledging the nuanced and complex currents within me, I am able to find compassion for both myself and others. I acknowledge the human frailty we each have in the face of the seismic forces of society: so much is uncertain and we know so little. If I try to find enduring waymarks in the changeability of our world, I find myself misdirected or confused. I can place reliance on very little.

If, instead, I place reliance on things valued by many wisdom traditions, such as generosity, kindness, moderation and courage, I find strength in the turbulence. I can aspire to act well, even as fissures open within communities and between countries, tribes and cultures.

Thinking geologically about our evolution, I am inspired to find a nobler person within me, just waiting to be expressed. And I know that there is such a person in you too: how might you give expression to this nobler self?

Contemplations

- How much energy do you invest in the way you present yourself to others? How does your self-image make you susceptible to being hurt?

- What unshakeable values are at the core of your being? How might you more constantly live by these, even when judged by others?

Leadership perspectives

In a landscape, the place we stand, the quality of our eyesight and the direction of our gaze combine to determine what we see. A similar process shapes the way we 'frame' an issue – our perspective depends on our position, the clarity of our thinking and the horizon we are looking towards. This section invites us to consider some of the ways in which we view the world.

Gaining perspective

The vision thing

Quiet industry

Gradients of change

Contemplating activism

Changing minds

Passing places

Crafting intention

Careless talk

Ethical edges

Light and shade

Rhythms and rests

Letter from Holy Isle

27 Gaining perspective
Written in April 2015

My first love and I met at university, where we were both doing maths. He specialised in statistics, whilst my passion was abstract algebra. After we'd been together for a while, he told me I was now statistically significant in his twenty-year lifeline. Be still my beating heart!

This came to mind because I've been thinking about scale and the relative importance of things. The context is the way in which humans can experience an event or issue as all-important and all-consuming for a few days, only to have forgotten it a week later.

A personal example is the redevelopment of a large industrial site directly opposite my home. In a period of consultation about the council's plans to build 100 houses, I felt a strong desire to put together plans of my own – and probably to move away. After a period of retreat, in which I contemplated the nature of change, I reframed my urgency to leave. In becoming clearer about how I wanted to invest my energy, the importance of the redevelopment diminished.

If you ever need to gain great perspective, consider the Heilbrunn Cosmic Pathway in the American Museum of Natural History in New York. It's a spiral ramp 110 metres long, representing a timeline between the beginning of the universe and the present. At the bottom, there's a vertical line, just a hair's breadth wide, corresponding to the recorded existence of the human race.

On this scale, it is clear that humanity is a fleeting expression of energy – and definitely not statistically significant in terms of the universe. A single lifetime is an even smaller energetic event and vastly more transient. On a cosmic scale, each of us is like a quantum wave-particle, appearing for a moment, then disappearing.

Leadership perspectives

In this context, events within a lifetime and, more poignantly, the thoughts and feelings of one person, are completely ephemeral. And yet, from within, they appear enduring and intractable. Each lump and bump of life, every pleasure, success, disappointment, decision and shame, looms large in our mind. Our perspective is skewed by the immediacy of our human experience. This is part of the hand we've been dealt.

I experience the volatile uncertainty of life quite acutely. As a child I threw a wobbly each year if my new sandals weren't identical to the old ones! In seeing my world as stable and unchanging, I sowed the seeds of an upset – and I continue to do this, well into my fifties. I'm sure I'm not alone in assuming life will be a certain way and then being frustrated when it's not.

So I've been practising 'zooming out' to help me grasp the flimsy nature of life and living. Watching a *Horizon* documentary on our solar system, I was captivated by a description of the formation of Jupiter 'in the astronomical blink of an eye – just five million years'. On this scale, my life has the tenure of a lepton or quark in the Large Hadron Collider.

The programme went on to describe how, with the recent discovery of many other solar systems, astronomers have had to re-cast their view of our own. It turns out that our solar system may not be in the steady state that science has assumed in the four hundred or so years since Galileo's time. Planets might change their orbits, in the grand scheme of things.

After all, if five million years is the astronomical blink of an eye, a mere few hundred years is too short to provide any usable data.

This change of perspective prompts me to reflect on how little time is available to me – and so think seriously about how I'll use it.

Contemplations

- What most occupies your mind right now? How much time and energy do you expend on this matter? To what end?

- In the context of a lifetime, how significant is this matter? How does this affect how much energy you choose to invest in it?

28 The vision thing
Written in September 2015

In coaching supervision, a client lamented that she didn't have a vision for her business. Two things flitted briefly through my mind:

- I'm not sure you're strongly visual in the way you operate; and
- Who says we need a vision?

As the client's narrative unfolded along different lines, I let these thoughts slide by. They reappeared later, when she stated an intention to be discerning in the type of work she agrees to do. I asked: what guides you in this?

We began to explore how a well-crafted intention might sometimes be more relevant than a vision. Prompted by my earlier transient thoughts, I wondered aloud if ambitions for the future could be described as soundscapes, or through texture, or even the senses of smell or taste?

Responses to this question depend, of course, on what we mean by *a vision*. To me, it indicates a direction of travel, a horizon that offers inspiration for setting out on a particular path. We can hold hopes and dreams for the way we want to live, as well as for a business. We might aspire to be a certain type of practitioner or to excel in our field. Alternatively we may seek to embody a way of working or a particular quality of spirit – and for these aims, the idea of a vision may not sit so well.

Vision has its place. I've embraced it often, most notably when, after completing my MBA, I worked through 'Drawing forth a personal vision' from *The Fifth Discipline Fieldbook*.[12] An image materialised, in which I was holding a book I'd written. With no such notion in mind, I got on with more practical things. And yet, a few years later, I began to write more often and then went to a couple of workshops. Eventually, about a dozen years after I'd envisioned it, there was a book.

So: 'yes' to vision.

And yet, nowadays, two things are evident to me.

Firstly, my mind can create an inspiring vision *in an instant* – and I later discover that it's inappropriate for my path and talents. I've abandoned so many sure-fire futures created in this way that I've become more thoughtful as to how and when I invest energy in scoping out possibilities.

Secondly, I believe that an articulation of *destination* needs to be consistent with the *nature* of the path towards it. My aspirations focus on the *quality* of the contribution I want to make as a coach, coach supervisor and dialogue guide. This brings my attention to fostering the values, practices, alignment and presence that support this purpose. My sense of *inhabiting* this future is textural, tonal, visceral. It's hard to describe in visual imagery, or words. But I *know* it, as an experience, when I touch into it.

This is the ground that was shaping the supervision work with my client. Her inquiry ripened into a heartfelt recognition that there is '*only* this moment'. Within this insight, she wondered how she could live her intention *now,* prioritising the quality of her work over concerns about income. She acknowledged that living this belief would require a *daily* (hourly?) leap of faith that she would be able to keep a roof over her head. And yet, at a cellular level, she was already deeply familiar with this expression of future potential for her business.

I know this uncertain place. Sometimes I'm able to make the leap, sometimes not. Yet, when I rely solely on 'a vision', I risk basing my future on what's currently in sight. This may exclude potential I can't yet conceive, let alone articulate.

Contemplations

- As an experiment, try reimagining your aspirations using different sensory frames. Which offers the most compelling connection to your future?
- How might you inhabit your future, today?

29 Quiet industry
Written in March 2017

For nearly twenty years I lived next to a factory. For most of that time, a rhythmic whisper of working machinery accompanied my daily life, punctuated by a piercing bell that signalled a change of shift every eight hours.

A couple of years ago the plant fell silent as production relocated to a nearby town. This made sense on many levels, for both the business and the village. Yet the quiet was eerie, especially at night – it took me months to acclimatise to the absence of sound. Meantime, nature began to reclaim the site – resilient bushes grew in nooks and crannies high in the brickwork, and flocks of pigeons, rooks and seagulls roosted in the beams and window arches.

Calling the jumble of edifices that made up the works 'the factory' disregards their provenance: they were built at various times, using different materials and methods. Depending on where you stood to look at the patchwork of production halls, plant rooms, warehouses and offices, you might have seen a uniform and rather ugly block, or a quirky collage of contrasting rooflines.

As I write, the buildings are being dismantled. The official term is demolished, but this word conjures a brutal destruction which doesn't reflect the precise and delicate undertaking I've witnessed since October. Yes, there are periods of earth-shaking violence – six-storey walls crumble and crash to the ground and palls of masonry dust swirl in the wind, covering the locality with a grey shroud.

Yet there are also quieter periods of housekeeping, where nothing much seems to change. The skyline retains a single profile for a few days while rubble, girders and other wreckage are sorted for recycling, or for building temporary roads and platforms to support the work of heavy-duty excavators and bulldozers.

The daily soundscape is a symphony of thunderous rumblings, toe-curling scrapes and screeches, and cacophonous clatters, booms and bangs. Occasionally, there's a pause – the machines are still and hard-hatted men assess the state of play with thoughtful concentration.

Overall, there's an air of quiet industry.

Clearly, there's a plan. Buildings are razed in an orderly sequence. However, it's definitely an adaptive process, adjusting to whatever is discovered as the fabric of each structure is stripped away. The piles of scrap are frequently reorganised around the site. The initial timeframe has expired, yet the work is incomplete, despite a benign winter. I imagine the plans being reworked daily, if not hourly.

The changes in my local environment provide a powerful analogy for the wider world, where established order is being overturned through war, exile or the ballot box. The visceral and visual nature of the demolition reveals the painstaking work needed to skilfully take apart an infrastructure and safely handle the wreckage. Sadly, as leaders, we tend to give (and get) recognition for creating things, rather than deftly dismantling what is no longer required.

In a time of questioning how we're led and governed and by whom, and as we unravel at least one union, we might ask: how will we treat the fallout of disintegration? The shorthand of 'the EU' or 'the UK', like 'the factory', masks a complexity of constructions assembled piecemeal over many years of changing circumstances. Disbanding such arrangements will impact in ways we don't yet grasp. Each business and sector will have things to unpick as well as new possibilities to realise.

I wonder how we might place greater emphasis on the quiet industry of the ground-clearing that establishes sound foundations for new ventures.

Contemplations

- What are you currently planning to change or create?
- What needs to be carefully dismantled to prepare the ground for your aspirations to take shape?

30 Gradients of change
Written in October 2012

I've recently been walking in my favourite Scottish mountains. Climbing hills is strenuous, and the steeper the gradient the greater the effort required.

In following a 'stalkers' path' up a Munro, I noticed how quickly I was gaining altitude, despite the circuitous nature of the path. Stalkers' paths were built to support the shooting parties of the Victorian gentry and they follow the contours of the hillside, rising in a measured way. The ascent is still taxing, but I stop less and arrive at the top energised. Paradoxically, in taking the longer path, I attain height more quickly.

In stark contrast, taking the shortest and steepest route up a typical Scottish mountain is slow and exhausting.

The experience reminds me of writing by George Leonard,[13] an Aikido practitioner and author. He describes homeostasis in the body: when we introduce change, we experience resistance as the body seeks to return to what is familiar and stable. Leonard asserts that this innate resistance is:

> *'proportionate to the scope and speed of the change.'*

Walking offers a visceral experience of this. On level ground, I feel a rhythm, an ease. I can match my breathing effortlessly to my movement. It's even possible to accommodate a gentle gradient without strain, as I walk regularly and am in good health. However, as the terrain steepens, my breath becomes laboured. I start adjusting my stride and my body seems heavier. Everything is more effort.

On the hill, I really *experience* resistance as I ask my body to make a change. The steeper the gradient, or the more quickly I try to ascend, the harder my body has to work. When I attempt to take the shortest route to the top, it is hard to sustain the energy required for any length of time. There's a mismatch between the capacity of my body and the gradient of the route and I stop frequently to rest. At the top, I'm depleted. Further, if I'm walking with others, my grim determination to make progress means I'm alone, mentally and emotionally. I'm separated from my companions by my personal struggle.

However, when I follow a stalkers' path, the interaction between my body and the mountain is a sustainable one. Working *with* the contours of a mountain uses more natural levels of effort and I enjoy the walk. If I'm with others, it's possible to remain in conversation with them.

This offers a metaphor for how we navigate change in organisations. When leading colleagues to achieve new heights, how much attention do we pay to the gradient of the required changes? What might we do to ensure that the effort involved in introducing new structures or ways of working is sustainable and allows people to arrive together?

I regularly notice leaders asking their team to head directly to an ambitious goal. This generates resistance proportionate to the scope and speed of the requested change. Minds may be willing, but bodies value the status quo. We can also find a parallel in resistance training with weights. Adding weights in small increments builds strength. Increasing the load too quickly risks injury.

And so, in leadership, how might we calibrate the scope and speed of future change? What if we invite all those involved to lay the foundations for a stalkers' path, a more meandering progress that allows time for everyone to adjust to the new circumstances? While this might seem slower initially, it creates the possibility of faster collective progress.

It's a long way around that is actually a shortcut.

Contemplations

- What offers *you* a visceral experience of the relationship between change and innate resistance to it? What does it bring to mind in terms of your experience of change in organisations?

- When next leading change, what kind of conversations will generate change in a form that takes account of human capacity?

31 Contemplating activism

Written in September 2015

It is a time of change, quite literally, as a cool Scottish summer shifts into autumn crispness, and nature begins the rich process of decay: matter 'breaking down' and loosening, distilling nutrients for future growth.

In parallel, I'm participating in a development programme in which I'm seeing ideas breaking down and loosening. The programme is U.Lab, conceived by Otto Scharmer,[14] and delivered as a MOOC, or massive open online course. Through a mixture of streamed live events, online resources and local learning sets, the programme aims to stimulate innovative activism and catalyse systemic change.

Supported by the Scottish Government, Scharmer visited Scotland for a launch event, which was brought to my attention by Lorna, a friend, supporter and former colleague. Lorna and I have been on many learning adventures together, and were excited by the potentials of this bold movement of activist energy.

Activism. For me, it's an evocative word. Until recently, and somewhat lazily, I was most likely to equate it to protests and marching. From a distance, activists often seem very sure of the rights and wrongs of their issue or field and, in a complex adaptive world, I'm wary of certainty and absolutes.

All of which meant that I was disconcerted when, last autumn, Lorna declared her intention to be more of an activist. She had been inspired by the wider revitalisation of engagement that had been kindled by the Independence Referendum in Scotland. While many friends are committed to, and campaign for, social and/or political change, it was the first time I'd witnessed someone making a conscious choice to engage more fully in such activities.

I tend more to the contemplative than the active. True to this, and

Leadership perspectives

grounded in my respect for Lorna, I noticed, observed and reflected…

A year on, U.Lab Scotland has broadened my network and conversations and refreshed my exchanges with established companions and associates. In one deep conversation, a longstanding friend commented that Lorna has *always been* an activist, introducing social change in the workplace. Even when it's counter-cultural, and challenges those senior to her, she promotes and embodies the principles of genuine engagement and collaboration. I agree wholeheartedly: Lorna is this kind of activist.

This realisation was a defining moment.

Slowly, it dawned on me that if Lorna is an activist, I might be one too, as we each have a warrior-like strand to our nature. I suddenly appreciate how often I describe, and speak passionately about, the relationship between the interior condition of a leader and the quality of their contribution. I recall that I wrote about this earlier in the year (see page 118) and realise that *this* is my field of activism. In everything I do, I endeavour to cultivate capacity, in myself and others, for integrity of spirit and for the courageous resilience to walk our own talk.

How does this kind of activist appropriately inhabit their cause? I don't know. To paraphrase the poet Rilke,[1] this is a question to love, until I'm able to live my way to an answer. I am readjusting my sense of myself and have no road map for how this will play out. Without answers, I have to live the experience, until a sense of meaning settles in me.

As I write, I remember that the award given to my book, *Pause for Breath*,[2] recognised 'literary and heartfelt contributions' to, amongst other things, spiritual growth, responsible leadership and positive social change. It seems I too am an activist – albeit a contemplative one.

Contemplations

- What is changing in the world around you? What is decaying? What is germinating? How are they connected?
- What ideas are ripe to break down in you? What might be nourished by this loosening?

32 Changing minds
Written in January 2019

Early last week, a friend sent an email: *'Am watching Brexit debate. Unedifying.'*

In response to this succinct appraisal of the parliamentary process, I rolled my eyes. Perhaps I should care more, but I seriously question whether our current political system enables people to talk about our place in the world in a way that reflects the complexity of that world. And so I disengage.

As politicians trade opinions, I reflect that I haven't ever changed my mind as a result of being told the same thing over and over. Subjected to this, I stop listening, at best. At worst, I dig in. Further, on no occasion have I persuaded others to see things differently by repeating my argument. And believe me, I've tried!

So, what kind of conversation *does* change minds?

When I've witnessed a shift in someone's thinking I've usually been showing interest in their perspective. I've acknowledged some positives in what they say and asked questions to better understand how they've arrived at their conclusions. To show genuine curiosity, I set aside my own position for a moment. In doing so, I'm *not* agreeing, but I *am* respecting their stance. After all, the view we each have is partial, in both meanings of the word.

I think of this loosening of mindset as an *amnesty of opinions*. As I free myself from the tyranny of my certainties, I create the conditions in which another person might do the same. Then, together, we may begin to find space to consider other options.

This is an inspiring possibility. However, truly parking my agenda is difficult, even when I'm willing. It's particularly challenging when caught up in debate, which is an exchange of point and counter-point, of proposing and opposing. When conducted well, debate is a powerful means of stress-testing a course of action, provided there is reasonable assurance about the consequences.

Debate is also valuable in comparing alternative proposals, again assuming a degree of confidence in how things will play out. However, it has little room for exploring assumptions or unknowns and so is less suitable for navigating uncertainty, nuance and complexity and finding a way to proceed based on a balance of probabilities. When seeking to uncouple the UK from Europe (or Scotland from the UK), this is surely the territory we're in.

Yet debate predominates – perhaps because it's a habit so familiar we're unaware of its presence? In the UK, we are schooled to compare and contrast, or to speak for and against a premise. We carry this practice into the workplace, as we make and evaluate cases for change or the status quo. Acclimatised to propose–oppose, we forget to ask if a different kind of conversation might better fit the circumstances.

A conversation that *does* create space for minds to change is dialogue. Dialogue is an attitude of heart and mind, rather than a toolkit. To prepare for dialogue, we consider how we'll *carry ourselves* into a conversation. We might ask: am I willing to listen sincerely to others, with respect? Am I ready to engage with an open mind?

Resolving to approach a conversation in this way is a good start. However, it can be hard to maintain our good intentions when the stakes are high. And building greater capacity to stay in the fray with poise takes time, which we say we don't have.

And yet, kicking the habit of debate and developing capability for engaging in dialogue may be the essential leadership work of our times. If we don't attend to this, minds will remain resolutely unchanged.

Contemplations

- When you have changed your view on a matter you held dear, what influenced you?
- How willing are you to genuinely listen to views that are profoundly different to your own? What factors influence your readiness to do so?

33 Passing places
Written in May 2014

The single-track roads in the north of Scotland offer a fine simulator for paying attention to, and reflecting on, our patterns of thinking and behaviour when we come face-to-face with someone with a conflicting agenda.

When two vehicles converge on a narrow road, how do we navigate a space that's wide enough for only one? As far as I know, there is no widely accepted convention for *right of way* as there is on water, so a bonnet-to-bonnet encounter is a wee negotiation, without the benefit of words. For both to proceed, one driver must use a *passing place* to create room for the other.

There can be a brief moment of intimacy when strangers meet head-on. Think of the side-stepping dance that occurs between pedestrians in the confines of a pavement, or between colleagues in a corridor. Each seeks to be on their way without bumping into the other. Such fleeting exchanges are a moment of connection, sometimes with a smile, a silent *acknowledging* of the claim each has. Without such acknowledgement, the encounter feels very different.

Observing ourselves in these physical encounters, we learn how we're likely to behave when opinions collide. If we tend to the view that our *claim* on a place takes precedence over that of others, we may find a similar trait in our conversations. If we tend to give room to others spatially, we may allow their voices to fill conversations and relegate our own voice to the side-lines.

Temporary physical impasses reveal our habitual tendencies more clearly than ideological stalemates. The story we tell ourselves about who *should* move aside is more obvious when two cars meet on a single-track road with passing places. There are, practically speaking, limited options:

- One person anticipates the situation and pulls over ahead of time – allowing the other to continue with minimum disruption;

- Both parties expect the other to give way, and when neither does… there is glaring, fuming… and an impasse; or

- There's a pause, while each driver checks for the *nearest* passing place – collective convenience determines who reverses and creates space.

In this last option, contact is made. Though brief, there is a genuine meeting, an equality of recognition, and this engenders a sense of mutuality in the decision about the use of the road.

Identifying a pattern in the way we deal with rival claims on resources or locations, we can ask: how does this show up in conversations? Dealing with conflicting interests in leadership conversations is rarely uncomplicated. If I have an aspiration for my team or project, what happens when I meet someone with an alternative claim on the same ground? What is *my part* in determining the *quality of contact* we make?

When opposing views arise in our conversations, archetypal patterns such as taking or giving *right of way* play out and some voices get omitted or overlooked. We give preference to the opinions of some people and discount those of others. In making assumptions about speaking rights, we impose or withhold our own voice. In each case, a conversation is deprived of diversity.

What if, instead, we strive to make good contact when opposing views are in play? How might we create metaphorical *passing places,* to allow room for manoeuvre? If we're able to pause for breath, we'll be more able to draw on dialogue practices such as respecting, listening and suspending judgement and so create *passing places* on the single-track roads of our conversations. In doing so, we may gain perspective and, potentially, find new ways forward.

Contemplations

- When you want to claim *a particular spot* at the same time as someone else – a parking place, doorway or seat on a train – how do you conduct yourself? How does this tendency show up in your conversations?

- When you next bump up against someone with a contrary view, how might you establish a conversational *passing place*?

34 Crafting intention
Written in February 2015

I've been thinking about the power of intention and its role in finding a coherent path through a messy and often unfathomable world.

Whether we are approaching a specific situation or shaping a more general mission, clear intention provides a bearing, a 'north' by which to navigate the many possibilities that open up, day by day, moment by moment. Without some reference point, I risk making random choices or not choosing at all. Then, later, I wonder how I got off-track.

For a specific situation, such as preparing for an important conversation where I know my views won't necessarily be welcomed, I craft intention in three layers:

1 Purpose – what is my personal agenda?

2 Relational – what are my aspirations for this relationship?

3 Systemic – what matters for the bigger picture and longer term?

This discipline of expanding outwards from personal priorities prompts me to think about what I really want from a conversation. It reminds me that I don't want to get my way at any cost, such as damaging an important relationship. It also encourages me to balance my self-interest and limited perspective with the views and concerns of others. It creates the room to change my mind.

The purpose and relational aspects of these three layers of intention are often quite specific to current issues and have some bearing on how things will turn out. However, the systemic aspect of intention is more *open,* in that it tends to relate to aspirations that are long-term, wide-ranging, interdependent or fundamental to development. Properly considered, it requires me to acknowledge that the eventual outcome will involve factors beyond my influence. The scope, scale and complexity of phenomena that shape what unfolds are beyond comprehension.

These considerations become vital when crafting intentions for a greater purpose, such as what I want to accomplish in my life, work or leadership. In crafting a *guiding intention*, I must be clear about what's in my gift and what isn't. In my headstrong younger days, I frequently exhausted myself trying to *make* things happen. Nowadays, I tend to frame my intentions in terms of my *endeavour*, without attachment to a defined *end*. In other words, I focus on the activities that I'll invest energy in, rather than the results I'm trying to achieve. In doing so, I recognise the limitations of my humanness: at any point in time there are potentials that I cannot even conceive, let alone express in words, and they need room to surface. If a guiding intention is too specific or closed, I may not notice opportunities that arise.

I see crafting a guiding intention as the first step in *a conversation with life*. When I've articulated the contribution I want to make, I *listen* for responses from the world. If my intention is sound, it is my experience that supporting events and/or people will materialise. In their absence, I must be wise enough to notice and regroup. The evidence will be there, one way or another.

This kind of guiding intention is a profound lesson in paradox: realising my aspirations is subject to the unfolding of a grand process in which I have barely a walk-on part. If I bear this in mind, I am encouraged to cultivate a sense of non-attachment towards what might be achieved. This creates space for greater insight into what is *actually* occurring. As a result, I'm less likely to exhaust myself driving a fruitless agenda. This learning is hard won – and frequently forgotten!

Contemplations

- What motivates you in your leadership? How might you craft this into a clear guiding intention?

- When next facing an important conversation, how might this guiding intention shape your personal agenda? How might you strengthen relationships and be in service to all involved?

35 Careless talk
Written in April 2018

In my work, I invite people to be considered in both what is said and how it is said. In life, I try to embody this and, when I put my mind to it, I mostly walk my own talk. And yet, in being human, I sometimes wobble.

These moments mainly occur when my attention relaxes or wanders – often at the end of a conversation (phew, off the hook) or near the beginning (not quite here/in gear). If careless talk is more likely at the edges of interactions, I need to sustain both attention and intention until (as I recently put it) I've completely left the building. By this I mean maintaining presence until an interaction is complete and all involved have dispersed.

Presence is a state that we all seem to recognise but is hard to describe. For me, it is about being available, and being open in both how I receive another person and offer something of myself. I believe presence to be both directional and qualitative. In being present, I aim to be clear as to my own intentions, and to offer my attention with energy that is inclusive and curious. When I'm able to do this, my conversations tend to be fruitful and enriching. When I forget, not so much!

Two recent events illustrate this. In one, I had a rare opportunity to have a face-to-face session with a client who normally works with me by phone. As we finished our work, we continued our conversation, carefully signalling the shift to friendship and shared interests. However, in being human, we overlooked a couple of factors that influenced our exchange: I am more up-to-date with the client's world than they are with mine; and she is profoundly interested in other people.

Stimulated by her questions, I talked a lot, relaxing into it. As we prepared to say goodbye, I casually remarked that I hadn't expected an inquisition! Later, she relayed that this felt like a criticism – which was not my intention at all. But in my tiredness, I accept I may not have given my friend the level of care she deserved.

In the other situation, I grumbled to a delivery driver who was picking up defective goods and bringing the replacement. Straight off the sleeper train, weary and irritable, I riffed on the inconvenience, additional costs, time and energy... blah, blah. I was not present, and lacked intention. I was just ranting. The driver got the wrong end of the stick and set hares running at his company – and I had to spend time and energy putting things right.

The pattern in these two events can be illustrated by my experience in a Leadership Embodiment[23] activity that explores 'being visible' and the feelings of self-consciousness that arise when we're observed. While those who are frequently in the limelight may become acclimatised to scrutiny, the rest of us often feel exposed and uncomfortable.

Personally, I feel 'squirmy' and my attempts to hide my discomfort range from brashness to coyness. However, with application, I can be on show with relative poise *for a while*. The activity explored this. However, as I successfully completed the task in front of the group, my attention slipped: I became awkward and graceless and blurted out something inane and self-deprecating – and then berated myself!

This brings to mind research that shows that most mountaineering accidents occur on the descent. The objective has been achieved and it is natural to ease off. This is when misjudgements are made.

While conversations are not life and death events, we will avoid the consequences of careless talk if we maintain our presence of mind until we're safely back at base camp.

Contemplations

- Reflect on the edges of your interactions: when you move quickly between back-to-back engagements, what affects how easily you disengage from one encounter and become present to the next?
- Reflect on some of your leadership mishaps: which might be attributed to an easing of concentration after a period of intense effort?

36 Ethical edges

Written in December 2014

It is a heart-stopping experience to watch extreme cyclist Danny MacAskill ride Collie's Ledge in the Cuillin mountains on the Scottish island of Skye. In *The Ridge*,[15] a small camera on Danny's helmet allows us to share in the vertiginous drops and the judders and bumps of the narrow rocky trail.

While the short film is an internet sensation, the documentary about *making it* is even more potent. In describing the toil and care involved in obtaining the spectacular footage, the documentary reveals the dedication and commitment required of the team. There can be no shortcuts in safely navigating the rugged terrain and changeable Scottish weather.

In one dramatic clip, the cyclist climbs the aptly named Inaccessible Pinnacle, with his bike over his shoulder. A watching mountain guide says:

> 'The drop on one side is overhanging and infinite… the drop on the other side is even greater.'

As I watched, I drew parallels with the occasions when we feel exposed in our leadership. Perhaps what we stand for doesn't suit those in positions of power. Perhaps we find ourselves in a moral or ethical dilemma, or facing a choice that disadvantages someone or something, whatever we decide.

In his cycling feats, MacAskill risks life and limb. As leaders, the danger is more often to our integrity or livelihood. At an ethical edge, what may be most at risk is our *sense of self*.

As a coach, I experience vertigo when a sponsor offers me lucrative work that sits uneasily with my values or practice. This is especially true when I'm seduced by flattery or the possibility of a higher profile. I'm also fragile when finances are depleted. The metaphorical ridge within me has:

- A drop on one side that involves saying 'no', risking the displeasure of a customer and potentially jeopardising future work; and

- A drop on the other side that compromises my sense of what's right.

This feels like a ridge between preserving my livelihood and my integrity. I need courage to keep my balance in such moments.

To ride this ridge, I clarify what's important in the long run. This provides an internal compass bearing that supports me to resist the lure of being pragmatic or expedient to maximise short-term gain. It also helps if I identify the qualities and values I want to live by, such as courage, diligence and resilience. I can then reflect on how to model them in what I choose to do.

Returning to mountainous ledges, MacAskill's mission is to make stunning films and find settings in which to stretch his skills and create something new. Even with his mastery, this requires enormous preparation and hard work. The documentary shows the early starts, the fatigue of hauling heavy equipment up the mountains, the practice runs, the re-takes, the relentless schedule of long, gruelling days, the slips, falters and falls. It requires commitment, discipline and spirit. The filmmaker acknowledges that it is scary work for both MacAskill and the team.

Whilst we may not risk life and limb at the ethical edges of leadership, riding a ridge between important values or issues is likely to be perilous. However, with the right preparation and practice, we can become better at keeping our balance on such challenging terrain. As we become more familiar with feeling exposed and unsafe, we can navigate narrow paths with greater confidence in our ability to make principled choices that avoid the extremes on either side.

Contemplations

- What does this narrative evoke in you? What are the parallels in your life, work and leadership?

- As a talented leader, what are you on a mission to 'make'? What will be the visible legacy of the best of your leadership? What will enable you to keeping stretching yourself and to continue making something new?

37 Light and shade
Written in April 2019

In *Let Your Life Speak*,[16] Parker Palmer describes a leader as someone with power to:

> *'project either shadow or light onto some part of the world... A good leader is intensely aware of the interplay of inner shadow and light...'*

To gain insight into the ways we affect others, he encourages leaders to engage in deep personal development to become familiar with our internal landscape. When we don't understand our fears and insecurities and the strategies we've devised to cover them up, we may inadvertently cause distress or even harm to those around us. For instance, when we feel small in ourselves, we may subtly diminish others in an unskilful attempt to feel bigger.

As leaders, we also delude ourselves. We may be ambitious, confident and knowledgeable, and be rewarded for these qualities. However, we can overplay them, or overlook their influence when we exercise power. Inner work helps us to be clear-sighted about these aspects of our make-up. This, in turn, makes it less likely that they will derail our efforts to inspire and mobilise others. In short, we'll cast fewer shadows.

We all have what I call 'foibles', characteristics that limit our effectiveness in certain situations or leave us short on options. Others might call such idiosyncrasies weaknesses or flaws. I tend to avoid this language because I believe that, if we see them clearly, we can turn them into assets. I don't see fears and insecurities themselves as an issue. It's our lack of awareness of them that leads us to unconsciously act to the detriment of other people or shared aims.

For instance, if I know I have a tendency to be sharply critical of other people's opinions (which I do), I can pay attention to the seeds of judgement forming in my mind. In catching an impulse to shoot first and ask questions later at an early stage, I give myself alternatives. I can open my mind and be curious about the way another person sees the world. Or I can offer my opposing view in a skilful way. In exercising restraint, I may discover new ground.

Palmer frames this type of work nicely. He invites us to become better leaders by knowing our personal 'potholes' well enough to avoid falling into them. We could simply ignore them and hope they won't do too much damage. Or we could try to fill them in – although, as on the roads, we may find such repair work never-ending. It seems wisest to study our potholes so that we recognise when we're approaching their edges. This gives us the opportunity to alter course.

I have a second reason for considering foibles as assets: shadow contrasts with light to create richness, nuance and texture. In accepting my humanness, my personal interplays of light and shade, I'm more able to be forgiving of humanness in others. When I see brightness and shadow as inseparable, I may remember to look for the light in a colleague or friend when I next focus on their darkness.

As I examine the ways my demeanour and actions shape my impact as a coach and leader, I become more equipped to consciously choose to illuminate my patch, rather than emit murkiness and gloom. In a world that feels properly broken, this small exercise of personal power feels vital to freedom and wholeness. When surrounded by shadow, we can choose to redress the balance by generating light or, as a minimum, refraining from adding to the darkness. Imagine the cumulative effect!

Contemplations

- In your leadership, how might you create more light today?
- What are your inner shadows and what will support you to refrain from adding to the darkness?

38 Rhythms and rests

Written in February 2015

In Scotland, February can seem to be the grimmest month – the brief, cold days are similar to those in December and January, but are unmitigated by preparations for festivities or the optimism of new beginnings. It is often said that the only advantage of February is that it is short!

This year, though, the weather where I live has been mostly settled – cold, yet bright and still. There is a quality of anticipation that is almost spring-like. It's a change in rhythm for this unlovable month and it makes it easier to notice that the days have actually been getting longer for several weeks. And, beneath the ground, preparations for a new season are advanced. Seeds, roots and bulbs are stirring, revitalised by the dormant period since their last fruiting or flowering. If only we could hear it, or sense it, the ground beneath our feet is whispering with gentle movement.

In nature, winter months are a time of rest and renewal. In contrast, human customs often call us to be busy. December seems *frantic* as we juggle a sense of urgency and deadline at work with additional social commitments and preparations for the seasonal holidays. The holidays, though pleasurable, are often even more full-on.

January brings New Year's resolutions and much *striving* to make changes: get fit, detox, launch new initiatives. We're seeking to *shape* ourselves, our environment, our work. Despite any benefits that accrue, many of us reach February depleted and weary. We attribute this to a general lack of light and warmth – but I believe the roots to be much deeper: we've lost the art of rest.

The need for rest is universal – life is a rhythm of alternating effort and ease: a heart beats as a muscle contracts and relaxes; living beings cycle between waking and sleeping; athletes train in intervals of higher and lower intensity. Rest is an essential response to endeavour, providing punctuation that restores energy. The contrast between 'doing' and 'not doing' allows us to calibrate the quality of our activity.

Periods of rest don't need to be lengthy, but in a 24/7 world, where work infiltrates evenings and weekends, we may need to pay more active attention to them. In reclaiming the art of rest, we might consider a different balance between longer holidays and shorter interludes like weekends. We could place renewed emphasis on brief changes in rhythm during a day, such as mindful mealtimes, walking between meetings, and breathing or centring practices.

The bottom line is that, if we overestimate our capacity to do without rest, there will eventually be consequences. One client refers to the 'stupid' days that occur when they work for too long at high intensity. To me, it feels like a hangover, a slump of energy after some overindulging.

The quality of our leadership benefits from good rhythms of rest. While there's no standard recipe, the renewal of leadership spirit generally has two features:

- Absorption in activities that are purely for enjoyment and pleasure; and
- Downtime to make good contact with self and to reflect, gently, on life.

Balancing something and nothing fulfils two functions. The *something* provides the rest associated with a positive change of focus. The *nothing* creates space to connect with, and process, matters we might otherwise avoid or ignore. It is, quite literally, time to catch up with ourselves and listen to the quieter internal voices that are easy to disregard in relentless busyness.

Together, the something and nothing combine to support us to attend to important stuff, enhancing the contribution we're able to make to the world.

Contemplations

- What form does genuine rest take for you? What is your optimum rhythm of rest? What difference does it make to your leadership?
- In your quiet times, what disturbs you? What is the deeper message? What needs to change?

39 Letter from Holy Isle

Written in March 2015 and first published in Coaching at Work magazine

On the Ordnance Survey map, Holy Isle, off the east coast of Arran, is roughly the shape and size of my thumb. On the ferry from Ardrossan, it's pointed out to me. It's bigger than I envisaged and more rugged, rising to a thousand feet.

Taking leave of the everyday world begins with parting from my car at the port and boarding the ferry on foot. Immediately, the pace of life shifts down a gear. Standing on the deck, Arran steadily approaches across a benign Firth of Clyde. Suddenly, a cetacean leaps clear of the water, powerful and fluid, returning to its element so quickly I wonder if I imagined it. A dolphin? A minke whale? I notice my desire to identify it, as if a label could augment such beauty.

Disembarking, travellers to Holy Isle cram into every available space on the local bus. Disgorged at Lamlash, we're ferried ten-at-a-time across a second stretch of water, packed tightly in a wee boat. Time shifts down another gear. At the jetty, we're welcomed by retreat centre staff. Wild Eriskay ponies glance quizzically and return to grazing.

We're here for a week of 'Joyfully Taming the Mind'. Our guide is the Abbot of Samye Ling Buddhist Monastery, who founded the Holy Isle centre as a peaceful space for people of all faiths and none. The sacred roots of the place run deep – a sixth-century Christian hermit, Saint Molaise, inhabited a cave on the then-named Island of the Water Spirit. The island was holy long before it acquired the label.

On retreat, periods of silence, teaching and meditation replace the distractions and busyness of worldly life. We also walk, talk, laugh and paddle in the sea. Each of us is more than usually confronted by 'self' – especially when in silence. Over the week, I bear gentle witness to my tendency to aggrandise, to my need to be recognised and applauded, to my insecurities amongst unfamiliar people and practices. These less lovable attributes are balanced by acknowledging my warmth, my willingness to listen and support, and my capacity to transform judgement into curiosity.

When, as a coach or supervisor, I see myself more clearly, my clients benefit. Difficulties in my work don't usually arise from lack of knowledge but from the way my humanness interferes with putting what I know into practice. Without precision, it's easy to overlook, or slide away from, the way I am contributing to situations that I find challenging. Naming or labelling such things is important to my inner work as a coach.

When I return home, Holy Isle itself holds me to account. Taming a small part of the island to be able to host retreats has taken twenty years of hard graft by many people. Slowly, the impact of climate, terrain, neglect and exuberant life-force has been moderated. Dilapidated buildings have been made habitable and land has been cultivated. Such endeavours are far simpler than taming an unruly mind. Yet, in my conceit, I often think that a few months of short meditation practice will enable me to work skilfully with the impact of losses, imagined or real hurts, confusion, fear and self-interest (to name but a few).

In reality, years of hard graft will be required.

And yet, beneath our human frailties, whether labelled or not, each of us has an essential nature that reflects the grace and spirit of a leaping cetacean, or an isle that is holy. And sometimes, effortlessly, we make contact with it.

Contemplations

- What catches your attention in this piece? What does it evoke in you?
- How might you describe the very best of yourself? How might you make better contact with this 'you'?

Leading and learning

In an increasingly unpredictable world, with non-linear relationships between cause and effect, our actions often generate unexpected outcomes. Such conditions invite us to be circumspect about certainty and to thoroughly examine our experiences to gain insight into what is shaping them. An important leadership attribute is to value reflective practice and encourage colleagues to engage in it. This section encourages us to create time to think.

Mind-taming update

Sweet spot for support

Raising questions

Mind the gap

Practice-based learning

Coming through

A gift of five days

The silent treatment

Back to basics

(DK)squared

Time in

Season of goodwill

Letter from Bhutan

40 Mind-taming update
Written in March 2015

When I left Holy Isle last autumn, I was inspired by the experience I'd had there. Six months on, as someone who is passionate about growth and development, it's pertinent to ask: what has changed?

One of the challenges of leaving a programme or event feeling uplifted and energised is that we quickly return to the existing rhythms of our life and workplace. Those around us re-enfold us into *their* patterns of activity, as if we haven't been away.

Despite good intentions to do things differently, the gravitational pull of familiar routines draws us back into the same-old, same-old. It's far easier to revert to a customary groove than to embed change. It's the principle of homeostasis: a system returns to whatever it knows as balance and stability.

This is what happened to me. And, as an independent coach, I don't even have the excuse of being part of a large system. It was dispiriting how quickly my heartfelt commitment to building a stronger meditation practice was subsumed by work. Busy with clients, I resumed the habits of my pre-retreat life. It was easy to avoid the graft of establishing new rhythms and behaviours.

The story might have ended there: I went, I saw, I settled back into comfort.

However, although my life and work *looked like* they were back to normal, beneath the surface the seeds planted on Holy Isle were germinating. Slowly, I began to realise I was no longer living 'the life that wants to live in me', as Parker Palmer[16] so eloquently puts it. Increasingly divided, I fell. Desperately needing to regroup, I arranged to go on a solitary, silent retreat for three weeks during December.

In retrospect, I wonder what unsettled me so much that it brought me to a halt. How could such a short time on Holy Isle have had so great an impact?

There was no single thing, unless it was the place itself, which seemed to provide an aperture through which I was able to catch a glimpse of a more complete self. In Celtic spirituality, locations where the separation of heaven and earth seems unclear are called 'thin' places. I sense that Holy Isle is such a place – in the world, but not of it. Touched by its character and energy, something profound shifted within me.

And yet, within months, my good intentions had dissolved. In fact, I seemed to be less able to function and began to make mistakes. What was going on?

I make sense of it by distinguishing between change and transition. William Bridges[17] describes change as situational, an event of some kind, while transition is the psychological adjustment to the new realities brought about by change. He says:

> 'It isn't the changes that do you in, it's the transitions.'

The glimpse of myself that I saw on Holy Isle was at odds with the patterns of living and working that fell back into place when I returned home. I didn't have the time and space to process my experience. And I didn't make the practical daily changes that would have enabled me to more fully integrate it. I'd done a bit of weeding in the garden of my mind but hadn't kept at it, and so my mind quickly became overgrown again.

The silent retreat allowed me to restart the process and to take proper responsibility for the work needed to genuinely make progress. During many hours of sitting meditation practice, I became reacquainted with the wandering patterns of my mind. With greater familiarity, I'm more likely to catch myself when I become distracted in the hurly-burly of life and to return my attention to what matters. In this way, I may yet begin to live more purposefully.

Contemplations

- How would you like to change your leadership practice?
- What routines, relationships and personal preferences conspire to maintain the status quo? How might others support you in making a change?

41 Sweet spot for support
Written in October 2013

Balancing challenge and support is pivotal to creating an environment for learning, development and growth. This piece examines the nature of skilful support, while the next looks at challenge.

What do I mean by *support*? In my dictionary, the definition of support is 'to bear the weight of' and includes: to sustain, to maintain, to back up, to nourish and to strengthen. A supporting actor plays a necessary secondary role to the principals, adding to the whole production without being centre stage.

This invites the question: in leading, how do we support those around us to thrive? This is an area of leadership that's difficult to calibrate. It's easy to misjudge the level of support that is required, and many leaders offer too much or too little. Too much strays into helping, advising or even rescuing others, and too little suggests indifference, insensitivity or even abandonment.

For my part, when I misjudge the support I offer a client, my intentions are usually good. I support too much from a willingness to share my experience, or too little because I fundamentally believe in the client's resourcefulness and resilience. Yet, when I make an intervention without testing my assumptions, I may be of disservice to my client, however noble my purpose.

When my motivation is murkier, the impact is clearer. In the early stages of using embodied approaches, I worked with a group where one participant was blind. Anxious and unsure of myself, I protectively partnered her in every exercise, discounting her ability to find her own way through the activities and compromising my availability to other participants. In providing too much support for one person, there was too little for others.

My best example of finding the sweet spot for support occurred while on holiday in the Scottish Highlands. There had been a fierce storm with gales and torrential rain and the following day brought a continuing downpour and wild winds. As I set out for a low-level walk, I noticed an inert, sodden, matchbox-sized blob on the doorstep. Closer inspection revealed it to have been a bat.

Returning three hours later, I was astonished to see the bedraggled creature trying to haul itself across the step. The sheer will to survive displayed by this tiny, waterlogged scrap of life moved me. What should I do? I could leave it to its fate – after all, nature is cruel. While a softer soul might have taken it inside, to warm, dry and feed it, I thought this would be stressful for the bat. Instead, I created a shelter from a latticed crate, shielding the bat a little from the elements. Without much hope, I went into the warm cottage.

Intermittently that afternoon and evening, I wondered how the bat was doing. Should I have done more, or done nothing? I resisted each impulse to check on it.

The next morning, I found the bat hanging in a corner of the crate, nearly dry. That afternoon it was creeping across the 'ceiling' of the makeshift cave. Later it was gone. Hard though it had been to leave the bat to its own resources, my support had been just right. My minimum intervention had recognised the spirit of this lifeform and its capacity for recovery.

This sweet spot for support seems to balance *listening deeply* for what another being needs and *respecting* their strength and skilfulness. In this *balance*, we provide a brief shelter from whatever storm they're in. In the respite, they can regroup and draw on their reserves and creativity.

Contemplations

- How well do you receive support when it's offered? What level of support is just right for you?
- In offering support, do you tend to give too much or too little? What is the impact? When you next extend support, how might you find the sweet spot?

42 Raising questions
Written in November 2013

This piece looks at the role of challenge in learning, development and growth and is a companion to 'Sweet spot for support'.

What do I mean by *challenge*? My dictionary defines it as 'to call into question' and includes: to make demands on, to stimulate and to check someone's identity. Sport offers a fruitful arena for exploring the nature of challenge. When an incumbent champion is challenged, they expect to be *tested*. We speak of *rising* to a challenge and of one competitor *asking questions of* another. Well-matched challenge stimulates growth in *each* player.

In contrast, when a person or team easily defeats another, darker language emerges: opponents are destroyed, thrashed or crushed, suggesting depletion and loss of capacity. A victor may experience momentary triumph, yet their skilfulness may be unchanged so there is no lasting benefit for them.

We can explore these themes in organisations, which are a form of *collective endeavour*. Challenge only makes sense if it *adds value* to the system. If challenge releases untapped potential, it increases organisational capacity. However, if it quashes confidence and/or impairs performance, it may diminish energy, motivation and resources. With the prospect of such vastly different outcomes, how can we ensure that a challenge is generative?

The quality of a challenge depends on:

- The *motivation and skilfulness* of the person making it; and

- The *readiness* of a recipient to receive, process and respond to it.

Motivation is a thorny issue. Challenge is often rooted in an assessment that some action, decision, behaviour or thinking is out of order. When we judge something to be wrong, bad, distasteful, stupid or poor, we *flavour* our challenge with correction, disapproval or reproach. From this place, *even when* we're thoughtful about the words we use and sincere about contributing to someone's development, an attempt to 'put right' can feel like a put-down.

On the receiving end, many of us claim to thrive on challenge. However, we usually have some unspoken qualifying criteria. For instance, we're often more ready to receive challenge to our ideas or decisions from people we respect than from those we don't. Further, we're often less receptive to searching questions when we're deeply attached to, or invested in, our view.

The difficulty with challenge is that, wrongly calibrated, it can damage relationships and lead to discretionary effort being withheld. In contrast, skilful challenge enhances working alliances, building collective capacity and resilience. Deft challenge opens new avenues of thinking and strengthens collaboration. Clumsy challenge closes minds and harms rapport.

To skilfully *stimulate* another person and *ask questions of* them, a first step is to shift our perception towards respecting their opinion or choice of action. We might be curious how they came to their view. What informed their thinking? What might they be unaware of? What might we be missing? As we reflect on *who* is speaking, we may find more tolerance for their stance.

We clear space to ask: what do I want to accomplish in making a challenge?

For example, if I want to increase shared understanding of the consequences of a proposal, and ensure that relationships remain constructive, it's unlikely to be helpful to embarrass a colleague by pointing to shortcomings in their work. However, if I ask for more explanation of issues that concern me, a colleague may rise to the challenge. They may offer new information, such as alternatives they've considered or their own qualms. This stimulates thinking in all present.

In this way, raising questions may generate new possibilities.

Contemplations

- When have you been challenged in a way that raised your game and supported you to provide greater value to your organisation or clients?
- What kind of challenge reduces what you are willing or able to say?

43 Mind the gap
Written in March 2014

Recently, there have been a couple of situations where I haven't met my expectations of myself, and I'm thoughtful about moments of error, failure, defeat, misjudgement or unskilfulness. I'm referring to episodes when, despite our general competence, effectiveness and good intent, we melt down or flare up, become forgetful of good practice or clumsy in implementing it. We only realise things have gone pear-shaped when the *impact* of our words or actions causes inconvenience or disadvantage to others.

Lapses in good practice occur for all sorts of reasons. Some are stimulated by things outside our influence. Others arise because we might have paid more attention to *this*, or to *that*, or handled ourselves more skilfully. The lapses that I find most illuminating are those I've largely brought on myself.

When I've made a mistake, or caused distress or harm, I draw inspiration from coaching clients who've met adversity with courage and humility. For example, one leader relied on verbal assurances from his team that policies were being implemented. His faith in his people was unfounded, with a real financial impact. Facing a deficit, he said: 'I'll never recover from this, personally or professionally'. Nevertheless, he committed to addressing the issue and improving governance. He also reflected on how he had contributed to events. Through this, his leadership matured. Soon after, he was promoted.

Which brings me to the bottom line: it's not a case of *if* we have moments of inattention or misjudgement, but *when* and *with what impact*. The measure of our leadership is how we then *relate to* and *learn from* the consequences.

When I examine the roots of my own lapses, I rarely find a gap in my *knowledge.* Mostly I've been unable to put what I know into practice. The issue may be situational, arising from the nature of a particular relationship or presenting issue, or it may indicate an underlying fault line in my practice, a pattern that, if ignored, will limit my effectiveness. Such fault lines develop because I'm quick to grasp ideas but am not always able to *enact* them. There's a *gap* between a possibility in my mind and my ability to *live* it.

For instance, when I read *Dialogue and the Art of Thinking Together*,[18] I was inspired by the profound conversations described. I wanted to be part of this kind of conversation. However, when I candidly examined my interactions with others, it was clear that my conduct wasn't always in line with my aspirations.

More generally, leaders have immense reservoirs of knowledge, yet it's harder to *walk the talk*. When we champion particular approaches, we generate trust and credibility *only* to the extent that our practice aligns with them. So, if we say people matter and then treat them shabbily, there's a gap between what we say and do. In this gap, our standing diminishes and trust is dented or broken.

Restoring trust takes time, attention and energy. It may be better to take pre-emptive action and foster trust by *more consistently* embodying our chosen frameworks, values and principles. This requires us to be:

- Honest about our shortcomings in putting knowledge into practice;
- Transparent about our inconsistencies and the impact of them; and
- Committed to the practice of aligning what we do with what we say.

It takes courage and humility to *mind the gap* between aspiration and practice. If we don't attend to it, the gap will widen. Eventually, we'll fall foul of it, to the detriment of our colleagues, organisation or reputation.

Contemplations

- What is your *pattern* of internal dialogue when there is a gap between the leader you *intend to be* and the leader you *are*? Do you:
  - search for someone or something to blame?
  - cringe and beat yourself up?
  - excuse yourself with a shrug – mistakes happen?
- How might you *mind the gap* and let others know you are aware of it, whilst exploring changes that will align your practice and aspirations?

44 Practice-based learning

Written in September 2012

Recently, British tennis player Andy Murray won the US Open. In 2005 he took Wimbledon by storm as an ungainly teenager. His raw talent was obvious, but his conditioning and discipline were patchy. Over the years, I've developed great respect for his commitment to enhancing his fitness, his versatility, and his mental and emotional resilience. It took him seven years of dedication, of examining his game and of doing whatever it takes, to fully inhabit his potential and win his first Grand Slam title. He is a model for practice-based learning.

I have similar appreciation for Josh Waitzkin, who has achieved international success in both chess and martial arts. In his book *The Art of Learning*,[19] he describes his development in each field. It becomes clear that he's *forensic* in his scrutiny of both successes and setbacks, searching to understand what he needs to work on next. He particularly emphasises *'investing in loss'*, almost seeking out adversity so he can learn how to navigate it. It's hard to cultivate genuine resilience if you only succeed.

These two young men embody commitment to improving their game. They understand the crucial role of conscious repetition in making progress. They also appreciate that generating sustainable change takes time.

What interests me most is the way in which people like Murray and Waitzkin deal with losses, hiccups in their game plan and environmental challenges such as the weather or questionable decisions by officials. They learn to recover quickly, to stay in the game. They later reflect on their experience, make changes and practise. They treat a setback as feedback that conveys valuable information about how to improve.

When our chosen discipline is leadership, we face a particular challenge when we try to develop or refine our practice because, typically, we have to do it whilst on the job. When we implement a new approach, it involves some trial and error, with variable impact: there's often a gap between our grasp of the potential of a new way of doing things and its messy unfolding in human reality. In the long run, how we relate to such gaps is crucial.

Furthermore, when we have attained a certain standing in our organisation or profession, we're more accustomed to being adept than to being a novice. Those around us, whether team members, clients, colleagues or bosses, assume we have answers. We're visible and our identity and practice as a leader are often held in place by expectations consigned to us by both others and ourselves. This can get in the way of making changes.

I encounter this most frequently when working with groups of leaders who want to increase their versatility and resilience in challenging conversations. Many become disheartened by a perceived lack of progress when they try a new approach and the results don't match their aspirations. For example, if we usually say 'yes' to every request for help, when we first say 'no' it may spark an adverse reaction such as anger or disappointment.

However, when our actions generate unexpected outcomes, even if they are unpleasant, we can choose how we relate to them. We can see them as failure and become discouraged, or we can learn to use practices such as mindfulness or centring to rebalance and create the space to see things differently.

A change in perception may enable us to stay in the game when we're challenged, surprised or simply confused. This is crucial if we want to embed a new habit, since it will take repetition and time. After all, it took Murray a lot of focused graft over many years to journey from promising newcomer to Olympic champion and Grand Slam winner.

Contemplations

- Think of a recent setback – how do you regard it? What can you learn from it?
- What might you change in order to handle a similar situation more skilfully? How will you embed such a change?

45 Coming through
Written in August 2014

It is the summer of the Glasgow 2014 Commonwealth Games and I've been watching the athletics on television. In one programme, commentators were celebrating great achievements from the past, including Jonathan Edwards' world-record triple jump in 1995. Edwards was present and, when asked about this experience, he referred to 'something coming through me'.

My ears pricked up – this phrase describes centre, a state of ease and flow. Curious, I watched an online video of Edwards' jump – he broke his own world record twice that day! In the first round, he jumped 18cm further than his previous record, effectively securing the World Championship gold. In the second round, he added a further 13cm to the distance – you can see a wee smile just before he begins his run. With the job done in terms of the competition, his movement seems more fluid, his landing lighter and softer.

Many of us have experienced this phenomenon in some form or another – occasions when everything seems to fall into place. Whatever we're doing becomes effortless, with impact *beyond* our expectations. We notice these moments because they contrast with our usual exertion, toil and sweat.

Our capacity for flow or centre is innate and it sometimes happens spontaneously. That said, what if we could increase the possibility of this heightened state occurring?

A perspective that might inform this aspiration comes from the work of JH Austin,[20] an American neuroscientist, who studied the *personal factors* that contribute to researchers making great discoveries in medicine. Austin proposed that major breakthroughs arise when *four forms of chance* coincide:

- Chance 1: blind luck – which may play a part, but with long odds against when deployed as a sole strategy;

- Chance 2: being 'in motion' – having a clear purpose and being active, curious, resilient and persistent in the pursuit of it;

- Chance 3: incubating a prepared mind – knowing the field, being observant and ready to think outside existing frameworks; and

- Chance 4: having other interests – allowing for cross-fertilisation from diverse spheres to spark new connections and seed fresh insights.

As leaders, how can we apply these principles to create the conditions for the extraordinary to come through us, as it did for Edwards in 1995?

An activity to enhance Chance 2 is investing time and energy in clarifying the kind of leader we want to be and what we intend to accomplish through our leadership. We might ask: how will I put my unique talents and attributes to best use?

To leverage Chance 3, we might aim to become more consciously aware of the *quality* of our engagement with others and/or our interventions in our system. Whatever our field and expertise, we can start to study *how and when* remarkable outcomes occur and examine the factors in play. Whether unexpected results are favourable or adverse, the same diligence and curiosity should be applied.

Finally, our leadership will always be enriched by having other interests and passions – as we enjoy any activity we take delight in, our creative mind will automatically make connections and offer up insights. We will also be happier and more effective, so Chance 4 is an all-round pleasure!

The deal, perhaps, is to find a *blend* of self-determining effort and being at ease. There is some evidence to suggest that easing off creates room for the exceptional to arise. How will we discern when and how to exert ourselves and when to take our foot off the pedal?

Contemplations

- How do you describe your experience when you're on fire – your timing is sweet and your aspirations are realised? How does this experience differ from whatever is more usual? What allowed it to occur?

- How might you attend to balancing effort and ease in your leadership?

46 A gift of five days
Written in March 2013

When I was struggling to attract participants into a leadership retreat, Julie, a previous participant, wrote a powerful blog post to describe her experience. She used the phrase: *'I gave myself a gift of five days.'*

There is something wildly generous in this statement: extravagance expressed as a gift of time in a busy, demanding world. In Julie's writing, I sensed that she cared *enough* about her own wellbeing, her clients and practice, and her loved ones, to face her natural anxieties about taking a step into the unknown. Then she found the courage to do it.

Generosity, care, courage: three qualities of the heart.

It takes a good dollop of each to sign up for a retreat, or other potent personal development experience. As I read Julie's words, I realised these qualities had also been important *for me*, at a time when I was offering a retreat for the first time. Approaching this momentous new venture, I had given myself *'a gift of five days'*. Despite financial challenges, I'd signed up for a leadership intensive hosted by Authentic Leadership in Action (ALIA[21]).

By the time the ALIA programme took place, my first Pause for Breath retreat was a commitment, rather than an idea. However, while I had a sense of the shape of it, I was a little short on detail and was beginning to be anxious that I'd bitten off more than I could chew. It was in this state of mind that I selected a module as a principal focus for the week at ALIA. I thought I would enjoy 'Embodied Leadership' with Wendy Palmer.[23] I also hoped it might resource me with ideas and activities.

In one of the activities, we explored our energetic alignment around a purpose or intention. The practice was to speak the intention aloud, whilst connecting in turn with three different centres in the body: the head, the heart, the core (gut or hara). The aim of this practice is to get a sense of the extent of our ease with what we're saying. As I did this work, I discovered that my heart and gut were at odds with the aspirations of my mind. While my headstrong nature was completely sure about the retreat, my heart was full of anxiety about what people would think of me. Deep in my gut, I was afraid I wasn't up to the task of leading the retreat.

Over the five days of the leadership intensive, with support from others, I began to develop a different relationship with the retreat so that I could offer it wholeheartedly and with integrity. I found my courage, generosity and care.

A key realisation was that the collective experience would be shaped by everyone who was there. My role was to *create the conditions* for the retreat, not to heroically take responsibility for everything. In this, I found my humility, gratitude and creativity.

In examining my own predicament, I also tapped into a sense of why people might hesitate to sign up for intensive personal development. Even if we crave time and space to pause, slow down and get some clarity about our life and/or work, we may be afraid of what we'll discover about our human frailty.

It requires an act of huge *generosity to self* to invest time, energy and money in doing inner work. We then need ongoing generosity to accept whatever foibles and idiosyncrasies we uncover.

There's nothing self-indulgent or extravagant in this kind of generosity. Many years on, my life and work are still being enriched by a gift of five days.

Contemplations

- Reflecting on your personal and professional development, what has had the most enduring impact and continues to shape your leadership?

- How might you give yourself a gift of time to renew your leadership practice, to the benefit of those around you?

47 The silent treatment
Written in April 2015

In his mystical work *The Prophet*,[22] Kahlil Gibran explores talking and begins:

'You talk when you cease to be at peace with your thoughts;'

In a period of silent retreat, I discovered this to be true. Journeying into silence was, initially, a relief. I was weary in body, mind and spirit and I drank deep, enjoying the simple fact that I didn't need to speak.

Easing into a rhythm of meditation practice sessions, supported by some T'ai Chi and walking, I quickly became rested. Yet, as my body and spirit breathed more freely, my mind awoke from dull exhaustion and was everything but peaceful. Committed to silence and without the usual range of distractions, there was no way to avoid my internal dialogue. What nonsense it turned out to be!

There's a Buddhist joke along the lines that, if you're able to laugh at yourself, you'll have access to immediate entertainment for your whole life. As my mind wrestled with itself, I did my share of laughing and had moments of compassion and gratitude, but I also 'did time' in a prison of self-inflicted drama, discomfort and dejection. Hurtling through this turbulence was like canoeing the rapids of a river, full of thrills and spills as my mind was tossed about by eddies, chutes and hidden rocks of its own making.

It was stark evidence of the human capacity to create turmoil without external assistance. Whilst on retreat, nothing in my daily routine changed, yet I felt different each day. It became apparent that, whether happy or grumpy, optimistic or doubting, agitated or calm, my experience was solely the product of my own mind.

I was sincere in my commitment to finding a path through this unruly interior existence and continued to adhere to the schedule I'd agreed upon, despite my restlessness. Eventually, I reached quieter waters. My mind began to settle. An inner silence arose, which seemed to incorporate a stillness that permeated my very cells. Silence became liberating and joyful.

As I reflect on this trajectory of relief, struggle and liberation, I recall a much briefer version of it. On a programme to deepen our skills, coaches were invited to explore the impact of being silent *and* still. The brief for the person practising their coaching skills was to simply listen and be still, neutrally witnessing the narrative of the person being the client. At first, my client enjoyed the freedom to speak, without interruption, sanction or approval. Then he became spooked by the lack of visual or verbal cues from me, as his coach.

It was hard to watch him grapple with his discomfort. The impulse to intervene was strong, but I kept faith with the brief. Suddenly, mid-rant, his energy shifted. He paused and deftly coached himself to a new insight and then fell silent. The silent treatment had released him to find peace with his thoughts.

If this potential arises from silence and stillness, what is the impact of the ceaseless noise and endless motion of modern life? In such restlessness, how do we find ways to be at peace with our thoughts?

In the extended silence of my retreat, thoughts became wordless. When I began to speak again, I had the sense of a voice echoing around the empty room of my mind. I was able to be *sparing* and *potent* in what I said. This discipline faded with time and my words became thoughtless once again. However, I am still able to vividly recall the experience of silence. And when I do, I speak less.

Contemplations

- To what extent are your words unnecessary? How might you say less with more impact?
- What activities absorb your attention and enable you to get respite from internal chatter? How might you make more time for them?

48 Back to basics

Written in December 2013

As a year turns, or an anniversary passes, it's natural to reflect on where we are, where we've been and where we're going.

Questions that begin 'w*here*' tend to evoke a sense of place and journeying. We could equally reflect on *how* we are, *how* we've been and *how* we intend to be. For some, '*what*' questions work best, favouring an emphasis on action, achievements and goals. Each type of question frames a review differently.

When I reflect, my focus is usually on what I've learned, especially in a period of personal and/or professional stretch. Review helps me take stock of the impact of any challenges and changes that have occurred in my life and work. It may reveal some next steps for continuing to mature in my practice.

If I think of myself as a vehicle for my work, reflecting on my experiences at the end of a year brings to mind a metaphor: stripping down an engine – dismantling it, cleaning some bits, repairing others, replacing yet others – and then rebuilding it and tuning it. I engage in this kind of considered process of overhaul regularly. Sometimes, though, I *lurch* into review, propelled by external events or a sense that something is awry.

It takes a certain amount of fortitude to scrutinise the way you work, but at least initiating the process offers a choice of method and timing. It's akin to booking a service for a car – you know that one or two issues will require work, but you're prepared. You can look into the areas that need attention and plan to participate in a training programme, or to arrange some coaching.

However, sometimes we take a car to a garage to investigate a clanking, whirring or other unexplained noise. It can be easy to ignore early signs of trouble, but putting it off for too long risks more serious difficulties later. The parallel in development requires that we notice and acknowledge our deficiencies and engage with them. This takes courage and resilience.

An example of becoming aware that something needs attention occurred when I was working with a small group of practitioners who wanted to use the approaches outlined in my book, *Pause for Breath*,[2] to augment their work. A key tenet of enabling our clients to embody dialogue practices in their leadership conversations is that we do our best to *walk our own talk*.

In unpacking my practice and explaining why I do what I do, I had a moment of truth.

We were examining how to use a framework that helps people to bring case-work to a group so that we ground learning in real conversations. As I responded to probing questions about this element of my work, I had to express things I hadn't articulated before. In doing so, I realised there was an anomaly between what I *said* I was doing and what I *actually did*. In setting up case-work to avoid problem-solving, I proceeded to be the most active problem-solver. I wasn't walking my talk.

I hadn't paid attention to this aspect of my practice, ignoring some unexplained 'noises' along the way. For example, occasionally a participant felt unsupported in the group or censured for choices they had made. This was not the purpose of case-work – but I hadn't looked into why it had transpired.

This insight prompted me to get *back to basics* and to take my practice apart, dusting down some elements, refurbishing others and discarding or redesigning yet others. Over time, I built a more congruent approach to case-work, to the benefit of clients.

Contemplations

- What are the key elements of your leadership practice? What is the signature of the way you work and lead? What might you need to refine or update?

- What have you been doing for so long that you no longer pay attention to it? What unexplained 'noises' are you ignoring? What is needed to address these?

49 (DK)squared
Written in July 2018

I acquired the phrase (DK)² from my friend and occasional colleague, Steve Marshall.[24] It refers to an aspect of learning – the phase when we don't know what we don't know. I've always liked the efficiency of it! I also find it useful in preparing for important conversations – when I remember that I don't know what I don't yet know, I lead with curiosity and a desire to hear how others perceive a situation, event or issue. For instance, when I talk to people about my dialogue work, (DK)² helps me to focus on understanding their context and offer meaningful links between the practices and their experience.

It also reflects my personal starting point with dialogue practices. Back in the day, as a director of finance, I didn't know what I didn't know. This meant I always played to my natural inclination in meetings and conversations: leading with my position. Advocating is in my DNA – and it's been strengthened by my education (which rewarded answers, not good questions) and workplaces (ditto). Working in finance provided further reinforcement, via the certainties that come with numbers, expertise and positional power.

Add into the mix that I'm rather combative and it's unsurprising that I spent a lot of time in conflict with colleagues.

I won many battles, but now wonder: at what cost? If I'd understood the value of inquiry, of actively seeking to surface, understand and respect differences, I may have been less drained by irritation and frustration towards those who simply didn't 'get it' (meaning, of course, that they didn't agree with me).

Yet I recall that, although I wasn't consciously aware of the distinction between advocacy and inquiry, I seemed to understand the principle enough to coach others. In 'Beyond words' (see page 42), I describe how I supported a colleague to draw out concerns about a proposal rather than blast her way through resistance.

However, I wasn't able to put this principle into practice on my own account! I'd go into a meeting intending to be constructive and collaborative, then quickly find myself seething with righteous indignation or disdainful incredulity at the limitations of others. I would simmer… then release impatient and snippy energy in a torrent of articulate reasoning. If opposed, I'd dig in and wield the weapons of my arsenal until others folded.

Whilst I may have enjoyed both the combat and the (fleeting) sense of triumph, it was an exhausting way of working and therefore not sustainable. In addition, people came to treat me warily.

And so, here are three things I wish I'd known I didn't know:

- How to press my point in a way that reduces the risk of implacable opposition;
- How to disagree in a way that builds relationship; and
- How to access composure and clarity when things 'kick off'.

While I now know these things, doing them consistently remains work-in-progress because my less effective ways of communicating arise from the foundations of human physiology. Regardless of my knowledge, expertise and good intentions, as soon as things get hairy the system of fight/flight/freeze takes charge. Instinctively, I attack, defend, avoid or appease.

It takes application and repetition to learn to work skilfully with such embodied tendencies. It's also a bit hit-and-miss: even elite athletes remain susceptible to tightening up in moments of pressure. Nevertheless, it's been powerful to discover how to organise my body and energy to enhance my conversations, especially when different opinions and interests are in play. And so, when I find I'm in conflict (again), I'm sometimes able to handle myself gracefully – with surprising rewards.

Contemplations

- What do you wish you'd known you didn't know?
- If you pay more attention to what you don't know that you don't know, what might change in your approach to leadership?

50 Time in
Written in February 2015

I regularly take time out on retreat, usually to regain a sense of congruence in mind, body and spirit. In retrospect, the experience might better be described as time in: a pause for breath that allows me to restore contact with my essential nature and with what matters to me.

During a period of time in, we may find new perspectives, reconnect to our strengths or let go of something that limits us. Fresh insights may emerge. We are likely to feel revitalised and better able to engage skilfully with life and work. Attending to the wellbeing of our inner world is important for our leadership in the outer world.

This principle is encapsulated in a much-quoted statement by Bill O'Brien, chief executive of an insurance company:

> 'The success of an intervention depends on the interior condition of the intervenor.'

It is clear how this relates to those who work as coaches or facilitators. However, it is also applicable to leaders and to anyone whose presence and practice touches and shapes the conditions in which people work.

Whether we aspire to transform systems, build or create new things, or support others to realise their potential, it seems to me that our *impact* depends on the quality and integrity of our *'interior condition'*. The spirit of our internal architecture flavours our thinking, conversations and actions, and so influences everything in our field.

I refer to this internal architecture as our human 'operating system'. By this I mean the suite of deeply coded beliefs, values, principles, knowledge, experiences and ethics that guides our ways of being in the world. It does more than this: the nature of it imbues everything we say and do, defining our unique personal presence. If we act with good motivation rooted in clear values and principles, those around us are more likely to respond well, even though they may not like our message. When our motives are murkier, that opacity may feel like a hidden agenda and cause confusion in others, even when they like what they hear.

The notion of a human operating system points to regular maintenance through personal development, reflective practice and processes such as regular coaching and/or supervision. These go a long way towards supporting the wellbeing of our internal structures. However, from time to time a more drastic upgrade is needed. Without this, we run the risk that the integrity of our inner workings slowly erodes.

How do we know when this kind of attention is required?

Perhaps we start to do uncharacteristic things, or become unusually distracted. Perhaps inconsistencies begin to appear in what we say and do, or we become inflexible in our views or overly strident in expressing them. Perhaps we find we're working harder and harder to less and less effect, or we're becoming short-tempered or unkind. Whatever the symptoms, deterioration in our interior condition eventually shows up in the external world, often to our own detriment as well as that of those around us.

When time in is due, there are many options: we can take a sabbatical, participate in deep personal development, engage in therapy, change our career or work–life balance. Whichever route we choose, it's likely to be both a significant investment of energy and money and a challenging experience.

It's not an easy choice – yet we ignore the warning signs at our peril.

Contemplations

- When you begin to fray at the edges, what are the warning signs? What activities support you to maintain your sense of yourself as a good leader?

- How do you assess the condition of your internal architecture? What might alert you to the need to undertake a more profound upgrade?

51 Season of goodwill
Written in November 2012

Approaching the festive season, I wondered how to support myself through a period when I'd be:

- Outside the comfortable familiarity of my usual routines;

- In close proximity to a group of people for an extended period; and

- Keen to have an enjoyable experience during precious time off work.

These statements could apply to Christmas, New Year or any similar celebration. With soaring expectations, emotions run high and, all too often, the raised energy spills into tears of disappointment and frustration, or worse. In the UK, we call this the season of goodwill. However, all too often the imagined 'idea' of the holiday founders on the reality of humanness.

At the time, I was actually readying myself for a trip of a lifetime to Bhutan.

As an inexperienced traveller, I was preparing for the adventure with trepidation as well as delight. I was excited because I've always wanted to see the Himalaya. I was worried because I'd been very ill on previous visits to Asia. There were many factors that might be unsettling: I'd be on unfamiliar territory, physically, culturally and socially; I'd have to adjust to a different time zone, high altitude and unusual food; there would be new people to meet and walk with; and we'd be on the move, in a small bus, for two weeks.

As an executive coach, I support clients to respond skilfully to the pushes and pulls of the workplace and life by using centring practices from *Leadership Embodiment*.[23] The trip to Bhutan was being led by Wendy Palmer, the founder of this work, and centring was part of the deal. But I hadn't expected to be putting in so much practice before I'd even packed!

All in all, I knew I'd be out of my comfort zone. In my imagination, I hoped to approach each wobble as an opportunity to pause for breath and recover my equilibrium. In reality, I knew my frailties would be revealed: I'd have to confront some of my less palatable traits and behaviours. Furthermore, each member of the group would be experiencing their own version of this. It was likely to be intense at times. Hopefully there would be some fun and laughter too.

Faced with the prospect of a variety of disconcerting events, there was one aspect of Bhutan that I *knew* I'd find difficult – the many dogs that run free there. I have a poor history with dogs, having been quite badly bitten when I was younger. How could I ensure my trip wasn't dominated by worries about marauding canines?

I decided to use dogs as a prompt for centring. Inspired by the season, I resolved that each time I saw one I would pause, centre and extend goodwill towards it. By doing this, dogs would become an opportunity to cultivate resilience, rather than a cause for concern. Thankfully, this strategy worked and I was able to fully appreciate all the wonders of Bhutan.

During any important trip or celebration there is collective pressure to have a good time. This brings me to the forthcoming festivities. I believe it's possible to approach the demands of any holiday by actively seeking to *minimise* the effects of things (or people) that bother us, which contributes to *maximising* everyone's enjoyment.

What is the recipe? The main ingredient is intention, a choice to accentuate anything that brings delight and to make light of whatever we find vexing. Season this generously with goodwill. Then do our best.

We might also ponder: why does goodwill need a season? How might we carry goodwill into the coming year and beyond?

Contemplations

- As festivities, holidays or celebratory gatherings approach, what (or who) might you find most difficult to meet with goodwill?
- In such situations, what ritual might you adopt to pause for breath, recover your poise and radiate goodwill?

52 Letter from Bhutan

Written in February 2013 and first published in Coaching at Work magazine

The silence in Bhutan is profound. I felt I could almost reach out and touch it – intense, resonant, forgiving. It seemed able to absorb any sound – words and talk simply dissolving into the vastness, transient and inconsequential. Since my return, the visceral memory of the silence sustains me in challenging moments, supporting me to listen for my deeper wisdom, for universal wisdom. After immersion in the energy of Bhutan, my ability to be present feels steadier and more resilient.

I went to Bhutan on a spiritual journey led by Wendy Palmer.[23] I wasn't sure what to expect – some travel by bus, some walking (at altitude), some meditating and some embodiment work for sure, but beyond the practicalities, what does a spiritual journey entail? Somehow I knew that this adventure would benefit me, my work and my clients, even if I couldn't articulate how.

In Bhutan we travelled from Thimpu in the west to Bumthang in the east and back again. There are few roads and they cling, precariously narrow, to steep, forested slopes. Our eyes were filled with mountains, forests, rivers, all on a grand scale. It was almost too much to take in.

We visited significant spiritual sites, many on crags and rocky outcrops, involving a walk and climb. We meditated in caves, in temples, on rocks beside a sacred river, in our hotels. I was often cold and stiff – we sat on the floor – no luxuries like meditation cushions! But somehow it didn't matter – the austerity added to the experience.

This theme engages me. The people of Bhutan have few of the material things that many in modern society regard as essential, and yet those I met exuded generosity and compassion. In keeping with Buddhist teachings, they seemed to have a sense of the connectedness of all living things and treat everything with respect. Despite material privation, I witnessed a spiritual and societal wealth that I found humbling and moving.

My journey gave me a taste of life with a little less: a little less food, heating, luxury (and oxygen). Amongst the Bhutanese, I found there to be a little less self-absorption, hurry and idle talk. Instead, I noticed more silence, sharing, graciousness and simplicity. Taken together, I glimpsed the possibility that the smallness of an individual life might liberate rather than oppress.

My experience of a little less was vibrant and cathartic and I wondered how I might embrace this back at home. How might I travel more lightly and pare back my life and practice? How little is needed?

As I write, some things have already been taken care of. It feels like my journey in Bhutan has wiped the hard disk of my mind. Quite a lot of taken-for-granted details are missing! I have developed a tenuous relationship with time which, for a planful person, is somewhat disorienting. Together, these changes have led to a number of 'dropped balls', mostly amusing, but one that resulted in the loss of a client. The benefits include a sense of spaciousness, so I'm being mindful about what I choose to put back in place.

In my coaching and supervision practice, I'm aiming for a little less intervention, hurry and striving. An immediate impact will be more silence and space and, in time, more acceptance, resonance and capacity to allow events and narratives to unfold in their own way.

I'm left hungry to go deeper into the silence of Bhutan, to do more walking and meditating. I intend to return, though I don't know how or when.

Contemplations

- Recall an adventure in your life – what makes it truly memorable? What longing does it evoke in you?
- How might you be more adventurous in your leadership?

'Letter from Bhutan' was originally the final piece in this book. However, one early reader, Sam Anderson, invited me to add something to balance the Preface at the beginning. And so...

Coda: Rejoicing

Written in December 2019

As I make this book ready for publishing, I'm thoughtful about things that have come to an end this year, things I've enjoyed or valued and perhaps taken for granted. A couple of working relationships foundered, a treasured piece of old tech finally expired, wonderful clients moved on, a publishing arrangement folded and, right now, the nearby swimming pool may be closed to local people.

We access the pool through the council's leisure scheme, in a complex arrangement with a hotel. In the past eighteen months, the two parties have twice been unable to agree terms. Access was withdrawn for a period in late 2018 and may soon be denied again. I use the pool regularly and sorely miss it when we're excluded.

So, as the year closes, I'm reminded that all things come to an end. Our hold on possessions is precarious, and our tenure in relationships is rarely secure. Eventually, everything we lay claim to diminishes, disperses, is destroyed or comes to a natural end. We can do nothing about this, bar accepting change with good grace and, perhaps, taking stock and regrouping.

This is easy to say. I find it much harder to put into practice, as illustrated by the recent loss of three mugs.

The first mug was reserved for visiting workmen because it wouldn't matter if it got broken. It disappeared in a kitchen-fitter's van, although he denied knowledge of it. I didn't mind losing the mug, but I was exercised by the man's duplicity, as he'd also ducked responsibility for other things. Judging him to be at fault, the absence of this mug lingered longer than was warranted.

The second mug was a favourite, a tall china mug with a design I liked. It expired on a very cold day, when the shock of boiling water caused a hairline fracture down its side. Natural causes, we might say.

Coda

The third mug was a gift from a friend and part of a long-running joke. It was particularly treasured and was shattered by my carelessness. I dropped a heavy pan lid on it and was cross with myself, especially because the mug made me smile.

Losing mugs is quickly remedied by acquiring new ones. However, we can also use such trivial events to illuminate how we respond to more serious losses. We might notice how we react when someone's deeds deprive us of something we value, especially if we believe they're in the wrong. We might reflect on what arises in us when we are thoughtless or slapdash and cause harm to a person or an object. We might ponder occasions when we attribute blame to others when, actually, something has simply run its course. Or we might consider how our experience of loss relates to our attachment to what is lost.

In reality, everything has an expiry date. However carefully we plan, manage, organise and protect, we cannot prevent this. But it may be possible to acknowledge transience more fully, which, in turn, may make the present moment sweeter.

Personally, I'm adopting a practice of *rejoicing* for the coming year (and decade). I intend to more consciously appreciate things while they are available. Then, when circumstances change, I'll know I've made the most of my opportunities. To begin, I recently swam 100 lengths of the pool. I'd set this goal a while ago but conditions had never seemed quite right. The possibility of losing access spurred me on.

And so, as you come to the end of this book, what arises in you? If you've enjoyed the book, how can you continue to make use of it to resource you in your leadership? And if you haven't found the book to your liking, please pass it to someone else because it may speak to them.

For my part, I want to thank you for your readership. It lightens my spirit and encourages me to continue to write.

Key terms and what I mean by them

The early readers of this work suggested that I include a glossary of some of the terms I use regularly as they may mean different things to different people. They added that it would also make my book more accessible to readers who are not (yet) familiar with my work. I'm happy to accept their guidance, with two caveats. The first is that this is not intended to be a complete listing of key terms – there will be others that bear further explanation. The second is that the descriptions that follow are not definitions in any technical sense – they are an attempt to outline my current understanding of the terms.

My intention is to offer a quick sense of the way in which I use the words listed, to give the reader enough context to continue with their reading. I do not intend to challenge or contradict alternative perspectives.

Centre/centring

Centre is an energetic state in which we are fully available to the present moment, in all its potentials and challenges. We are in tune with our situation and environment, and draw on the energies around us to be of service to all involved. In this state we act and speak with ease, confidence and insight. We are connected, compassionate and courageous. It is a state in which we are inspired and inspiring. It can also be described as being in flow, or in the zone.

It may also be helpful to understand centre in contrast to our everyday self, in which we tend to be on autopilot, using tried and tested approaches because we don't have enough time to think. In this state we are also prone to taking things personally and behaving in predictable ways. This is simply part of being human and is good enough for much of what we do. But sometimes, when facing a situation that is both important and delicate, we benefit from

Key terms

having the capacity to go beyond our everyday self and to risk responding in a new way.

Centring practice

A centring practice is a sequence of adjustments to physiology, mind, spirit and energy that creates conditions in which it is more likely that centre will occur. In doing a centring practice, we first stabilise ourselves and then become open and receptive to others and to events. Even if we don't fully access centre, a centring practice will invoke an attitude that is more resourceful and responsive than either doing nothing or simply cracking on! There are many different approaches to centring. The one I use most often comes from the Leadership Embodiment practices developed by Wendy Palmer[23] as I am accredited in her approach.

Dialogue

William Isaacs[18] wrote:

> *'Dialogue is a conversation with center, not sides.'*

Dialogue is a word that is used in many different ways, with a variety of meanings. When I use it, I do so deliberately, and always in the context of the body of work begun by the physicist David Bohm, and then developed and made tangible by practitioners and thought leaders such as Peter Garrett and Jane Ball, and academics such as William Isaacs, Otto Scharmer and others at MIT (Massachusetts Institute of Technology).

I have written a whole book about what I mean by dialogue and may write another. Here I will simply say it is a conversation in which we truly connect with others and explore challenging ground together in order to gain some shared understanding. It is a conversation in which we listen, we are curious, we respect each other and we speak with frankness. It is also a conversation in which we suddenly realise that several hours have passed! At its best, it is a collective energetic state akin to centre.

Again, it is helpful to understand dialogue in contrast to other types of conversation. It is not a set of tools or techniques that enables us to be more skilful in getting what we want from a conversation. It is a way of being, a way of carrying ourselves and relating to others. Dialogue is a conversation in which we willingly engage in the struggle of understanding the minds and hearts of others.

Leadership

I try to talk about leadership rather than leaders because I tend to mean the acts of bringing out the best in ourselves and others, and of finding a good response to any presenting situation, regardless of whether we hold a position of seniority. I believe that leadership begins with self: holding ourselves to account, continuing to learn and keeping ourselves healthy in mind, body and spirit. When we have that nailed, we might encourage others to do the same.

I think that leadership is about stature and standing, rather than status and station. I see leadership in support staff who find the courage to speak out when things are not right. I see leadership in those who meet the most adverse events with grace. I see leadership in those who *do* hold positions of power, yet have the humility to admit that they don't have answers, listening to others without judgement and being willing to change their minds. In my view, leadership starts with acknowledging our shared humanity and contributing in a way that serves others.

Mindfulness

Mindfulness is a word that has become widely used. It has many meanings and, in current times, often refers to a particular set of practices that supports the settling of mind in preparation for meditation.

I use the word more generally, in a way that means being aware of our thoughts, feelings and options for speech and action. For me, a key question is: mindfulness of what? To be mindful is to notice, without taking issue or sides. It is to be aware of what is happening as it is happening, with a sense of both compassion and dispassion. It is to become familiar with our habits of thought and deed and to ask how well they are serving us in *this* moment. Being mindful creates a moment of choice, so we can be more deliberate in what we say and do.

Acknowledgements and gratitude

How many people does it take to publish a book? Many more than I ever imagined. I was held afloat by the generosity of those who invested time and energy in challenge and/or support. Thank you.

For contributions of insight and wisdom on reading early drafts: Chris Bowring, Susan Burney, Caren Gilbert, Dr Alison Williams, Claire Whitelaw, Jill Young DL. Your insights radically reshaped the book.

For reading later drafts and encouraging me to believe: Sam Anderson, Liz Archibald, Aileen Brown, Cath Denholm, Oonagh Gil, Heather Sim and the many others who offered moral support and cheered me on in the drawn-out process to get this one to press.

For those from whom I learned on-the-job: my coaching and supervision clients, members of my dialogue practice development groups and participants in my Pause for Breath retreats.

For her design and layout expertise: Bek Pickard.

For their part in the original publication of this book: the editing and digital teams at Matador.

References

1. *Letters to a Young Poet*, Rainer Maria Rilke, WW Norton and Company, October 1993

2. *Pause for Breath: Bringing the practices of mindfulness and dialogue to leadership conversations*, Amanda Ridings, Matador, January 2020 (first published by Live-it Publishing, July 2011)

3. www.originate.org.uk

4. *The Invitation*, Oriah Mountain Dreamer, Element Books, May 2000

5. *Unlikely Teachers*, Judy Ringer, One Point Press, April 2006

6. https://andrew-greig.weebly.com/biography.html

7. *Preferred Lies*, Andrew Greig, W&N; New Ed edition, April 2007

8. *At the Loch of the Green Corrie*, Andrew Greig, Quercus Publishing Ltd, March 2011

9. https://eu.themyersbriggs.com/en/tools/MBTI/MBTI-personality-Types

10. *The Te of Piglet*, Benjamin Hoff, Penguin, February 1994

11. *The World Café*, Juanita Brown et al., Berrett-Koehler Publishers, May 2005

12. *The Fifth Discipline Fieldbook*, Senge et al., Nicholas Brealey Publishing, June 1994

13. *Mastery*, George Leonard, Penguin, February 1992

14. *Theory U: Leading from the Future as It Emerges*, C. Otto Scharmer, Berrett-Koehler Publishers, August 2016

15. https://www.youtube.com/watch?v=xQ_IQS3VKjA

16. *Let Your Life Speak: Listening for the Voice of Vocation*, Parker J. Palmer, Jossy Bass, September 1999

17. *Managing Transitions: Making the Most of Change*, William Bridges, Nicholas Brealey Publishing, November 2003

18. *Dialogue and the Art of Thinking Together*, William Isaacs, Doubleday, May 1999

19. *The Art of Learning: An Inner Journey to Optimal Performance*, Josh Waitzkin, Free Press, July 2008

20. *Management Research: An Introduction*, Mark Easterby-Smith et al., SAGE Publications Ltd, 1991

21. ALIA's activities are now part of Naropa University: https://www.naropa.edu/academics/alc/index.php

22. *The Prophet*, Kahlil Gibran, Pan Books, 1991

23. *Leadership Embodiment: How the Way We Sit and Stand Can Change the Way We Think and Speak*, Wendy Palmer & Janet Crawford, CreateSpace Independent Publishing Platform, October 2013

24. www.drstevemarshall.com

About the author

Based in the Cairngorms National Park in Scotland, Amanda Ridings is an executive coach, coach supervisor and T'ai Chi practitioner. In all her work, she fosters the embodiment of dialogue practices and enables those caught up in relentless activity to pause for breath and clarify their leadership purpose. To learn more about Amanda's work and experiences, find her on LinkedIn.

Also by Amanda Ridings:

Pause for Breath gained a Silver Nautilus Award in 2012, in the category of Conscious Business and Leadership. Nautilus Awards aim to recognise exceptional literary contributions to fields such as spiritual growth, responsible leadership and positive social change.

Pause for Breath is for leaders, coaches and practitioners who are intrigued by their contribution to, and impact on, conversations, and who are committed to cultivating an authentic presence and voice.

The book explores:

- the influence of internal dialogue on your interactions with others and your effectiveness in your organisation;

- how to increase your versatility in challenging or delicate conversations and to develop capacity for doing this in 'bad weather' (adverse conditions); and

- how to germinate systemic change, one leadership conversation at a time.

www.ingramcontent.com/pod-product-compliance
Lightning Source LLC
Chambersburg PA
CBHW061154010526
44118CB00027B/2965